Oracle Certification Prep

Study Guide for

1Z0-146: Oracle Database 11g:

Advanced PL/SQL

Matthew Morris

Study Guide for Oracle Database 11g: Advanced PL/SQL (Exam 1Z0-146) Rev 1.0

Copyright @ 2013 by Matthew Morris. All rights reserved. Except as permitted under the Copyright Act of 1976, no part of this publication may be reproduced or distributed in any form or by any means, or stored in a database or retrieval system, without the prior written permission of the Author.

Oracle is a registered trademark of Oracle Corporation and/or its affiliates.

Information has been obtained by the Author from sources believed to be reliable. However, because of the possibility of human or mechanical error by the sources, Author, or others, Author does not guarantee to the accuracy, adequacy, or completeness of any information included in this work and is not responsible for any error or omissions or the results obtained from the use of such information.

Oracle Corporation does not make any representations or warranties as to the accuracy, adequacy, or completeness of any information included in this work and is not responsible for any errors or omissions or the results obtained from the use of such information.

ISBN-13: 978-1482570748
ISBN-10: 1482570742

Oracle Certification Prep

Table of Contents

What to Expect from the Test 8

What to Expect from this Study Guide 9

Additional Study Resources 11

Oracle11g: Advanced PL/SQL 12

    Introduction to PL/SQL 12

PL/SQL Programming Concepts: Review 20

    List restrictions on calling functions from SQL expressions 20

    Handle exceptions 20

    Manage dependencies 26

    Use Oracle-supplied packages 29

Designing PL/SQL Code 34

    Identify guidelines for cursor design 34

    Use cursor variables 41

    Create subtypes based on existing types 46

Working with Collections 50

    Create collections 50

    Use collection methods 58

    Manipulate collections 62

    Distinguish between the different types of collections and their uses .. 67

Using Advanced Interface Methods 70

    Execute external C programs from PL/SQL 70

    Execute Java programs from PL/SQL 73

Implementing Fine-Grained Access Control for VPD 75

Explain the process of fine-grained access control 75

Implement and test fine-grained access control 78

Manipulating Large Objects 84

Create and manage LOB data types 84

Use the DBMS_LOB PL/SQL package 90

Use of temporary LOBs 96

Administering SecureFile LOBs 99

Describe SecureFile LOB features 99

Enable SecureFile LOB deduplication, compression, and encryption .. 101

Migrate BasicFile LOBs to the SecureFile LOB format 107

Performance and Tuning 114

Use native and interpreted compilation methods 114

Tune PL/SQL code 116

Enable Intraunit inlining 121

Improving Performance with Caching 126

Improve memory usage by caching SQL result sets and using the DBMS_RESULT_CACHE package 126

Write queries that use the result cache hint 128

Set up PL/SQL functions to use PL/SQL result caching 131

Analyzing PL/SQL Code 134

Run reports on source code 134

Determine identifier types and usages 139

Use DBMS_METADATA to retrieve object definitions 141

Profiling and Tracing PL/SQL Code 144

Trace PL/SQL program execution 144

Profile PL/SQL applications 149

Safeguarding Your Code Against SQL Injection Attacks 155

Describe SQL injections 155

Reduce attack surfaces 157

Use DBMS_ASSERT 158

Design immune code 160

Test code for SQL injection flaws 162

What to Expect from the Test

The test consists of 68 multiple choice or multiple answer questions. The passing score listed on Oracle Education at this time is 65%, but as with all Oracle certification tests, they note it is subject to change. This test contains a large number of questions that contain one or more exhibits.

As you would expect, in this exam you're going to be looking at a significant number of PL/SQL constructs. Many, possibly most, questions that reference PL/SQL will ask if the code generates an error, and if so, why. I find these to be some of the worst questions to answer. You have to be able to rapidly scan code that you didn't write, determine what each statement does, and that the syntax is all correct. Each time I answer one of these questions, I'm always concerned that I read over the code too quickly and missed a flaw. That makes me tend to spend too much time on them... which is a bad thing. Because it is necessary to have written a good bit of code in order to recognize errors without having a compiler handy, these questions will trip up people that have not written much PL/SQL. This is a good result from the viewpoint of Oracle Education's intention for this particular test.

The questions on the test seemed to be spread fairly evenly among all of the topics mentioned by Oracle Education (and covered in this guide). I didn't notice a slant towards any one topic. Several of the questions had what I considered to be tricky wording. One I looked at for several minutes thinking that none of the answers was correct until I re-read the question and saw how the wording constrained the possible correct answers.

On many Oracle exams, I have found that the exhibits are not always required to answer the question. For this exam, I have to say that they were almost always required viewing. Read the questions completely, examine the code carefully and look at all of the answer before making your choice. That said, pay close attention to the time. With ninety minutes to answer 68 questions, you have just under eighty seconds per question. Spend your time efficiently. Do not rush your answers, but make sure you don't run out of time before running out of questions. This test does not have the massive time crunch that 1Z0-144 did, but the questions are a good bit harder and require more 'think' time. Any questions you leave unanswered are automatically wrong.

What to Expect from this Study Guide

This document is built around the subject matter topics that Oracle Education has indicated will appear on the 1Z0-146 exam. I've gathered together material from several Oracle documentation sources and created numerous code examples. Together they should help to familiarize you with the PL/SQL concepts, logic, and syntax that you will need to answer the questions you're likely to see on the test. Be aware that reading this guide is not going to make you into a PL/SQL programmer, nor is it supposed to. There are books available that are designed to improve your skills and knowledge as a PL/SQL developer. This guide is designed to help you to pass the 1Z0-146 certification exam.

If you are planning to take this exam, then the assumption is that you already have significant experience coding in PL/SQL. If you do not, then you need to examine the reasons you are pursuing this particular test. Passing it won't make you an expert PL/SQL programmer, but it may raise the expectations of anyone who hires you. If nothing else, you had better plan on spending a lot of time studying and even more time practicing writing code. Reading about code can only do so much for you. You must write code in order to become an expert. Typing in the examples from books doesn't count. When studying for this test, or any test, I recommend that you use as many sources of information as possible. I have linked to a number of freely available white papers and articles in the companion website mentioned in the next section. You should download and install Oracle XE so that you can get as much hands-on experience writing code as possible. When you are using this guide, do not simply read the text, glance at the code long enough to say to yourself 'Yep, that looks like code' and then move on to the next paragraph. The code is the meat of this exam. You must understand both the syntax and the logic of the PL/SQL functionality that will be on the exam. Type it in to your Oracle XE database. Compile it. Change it. See how many different errors you can get. You learn more from doing something wrong that you do from getting it right the first time.

The goal of this guide is to present to you the concepts and information most likely to be the subject of test questions, and to do so in a very compact format that will allow you to read through it more than once to reinforce the information. If much of what is presented in this guide is over your head, then you need to supplement it with other sources of study materials. If you have significant knowledge of PL/SQL concepts and are an experienced PL/SQL developer, then this book will help to reinforce your knowledge in the areas you will need the most. If you have minimal experience with PL/SQL, the compressed format of this guide is not likely to be the best method for learning. It is possible (barely) that it will provide you with sufficient information to pass the test, but you will have major deficiencies as a PL/SQL developer.

Additional Study Resources

The companion website to this series is www.oraclecertificationprep.com. The site contains many additional resources that can be used to study for this exam (and others). From the entry page of the website, click on the 'Exams' button, and then select the link for this test. The Exam Details page contains links to the following information sources:

- Applicable Oracle documentation.
- Third-party books relevant to the exam.
- White papers and articles on Oracle Learning Library on topics covered in the exam.
- Articles on the Web that may be useful for the exam.

The website will <u>never</u> link to unauthorized content such as brain dumps or illegal content such as copyrighted material made available without the consent of the author. I cannot guarantee the accuracy of the content links. While I have located the data and scanned it to ensure that it is relevant to the given exam, I did not write it and have not proofread it from a technical standpoint. The material on the Oracle Learning Library is almost certain to be completely accurate and most of the other links come from highly popular Oracle support websites and are created by experienced Oracle professionals.

I recommend that you use more than one source of study materials whenever you are preparing for a certification. Reading information presented from multiple different viewpoints can help to give you a more complete picture of any given topic. The links on the website can help you to do this. Fully understanding the information covered in this certification is not just valuable so that getting a passing score is more likely – it will also help you in your career. I guarantee that in the long run, any knowledge you gain while studying for this certification will provide more benefit to you than any piece of paper or line on your resume.

Oracle11g: Advanced PL/SQL

Introduction to PL/SQL

PL/SQL adds the processing power of a procedural language to the data-manipulating capability of SQL. PL/SQL provides procedural constructs, such as conditional statements and loops that cannot be performed using standard SQL. It provides the ability to declare variables and constants, control program flow, define subprograms, and handle runtime errors. Complex problems can be broken down into discrete subprograms, which can be reused in multiple applications. SQL data manipulation language (DML) statements can be directly entered inside PL/SQL blocks, and it is possible to use subprograms to execute data definition language (DDL) and Data Control Language (DCL) statements.

PL/SQL is tightly integrated with SQL and allows you to make use of all of the SQL capabilities. You can execute SQL data manipulation, cursor control, and transaction control statements. PL/SQL can use existing SQL functions, operators, and pseudocolumns and it fully supports SQL data types without any need for conversion. Through the use of collections, bind variables, and cached programs, PL/SQL can reduce network traffic, SQL parse operations and other overhead, improving performance on the database. Once developed, PL/SQL applications can be run on any operating system and platform where Oracle Database runs.

A block is the basic unit of a PL/SQL program. PL/SQL blocks group related declarations and statements. The four keywords that define a PL/SQL block are: DECLARE, BEGIN, EXCEPTION, and END. They are used to make up the three sections of a block:

- **DECLARE** -- The declarative section begins with the keyword DECLARE and ends when the executable section starts. This section is optional and is used to declare variables, constants, cursors, and user-defined data types.
- **BEGIN** -- The executable section of the block starts with the BEGIN keyword and ends with the END keyword. This is the only mandatory section of a PL/SQL block and must contain at least

one statement. The executable section can contain an effectively unlimited number of PL/SQL blocks. This section contains the meat of the PL/SQL program.
- **EXCEPTION** -- The exception-handling section is used to trap and handle run-time errors. It begins with the EXCEPTION keyword and ends with the END keyword. This section is optional.

PROCEDURES

A stored procedure is a subprogram that performs a specific action. Procedures must be declared and defined before they can be invoked. It is possible to declare it first and then define it later in the same block, subprogram, or package. Alternately it can be declared and defined at the same time. Procedures can accept parameters, update parameters and generate a return value. They are not required to do any of these. The basic syntax to create a procedure is:

```
CREATE [OR REPLACE] PROCEDURE procedure_name
      [(argument1  [mode1]   datatype1,
        Argument2  [mode2]   datatype2,
        ...)]
IS|AS
BEGIN
  procedure_body;
END [procedure_name];
```

The following is a simple procedure. When supplied a date value as a parameter (presumably a birth date), it calculates the next birthday and what day of the week it is on. Procedures are called as statements from within PL/SQL as the anonymous blocks after the procedure demonstrate.

```
CREATE OR REPLACE PROCEDURE birthday(p_birthdate   DATE)
IS
  v_next_bday     DATE;
BEGIN
  v_next_bday := TO_DATE(TO_CHAR(p_birthdate, 'DD-MON') ||
                         TO_CHAR(SYSDATE, 'YY'));

  IF v_next_bday < SYSDATE THEN
    v_next_bday := ADD_MONTHS(v_next_bday, 12);
  END IF;

  DBMS_OUTPUT.PUT_LINE('Your next birthday is: ' ||
                       TO_CHAR(v_next_bday, 'DD-MON-YY'));

  DBMS_OUTPUT.PUT_LINE('It''s on a ' ||
                       TO_CHAR(v_next_bday, 'Day'));

END;


BEGIN
  birthday('14-SEP-72');
END;

Your next birthday is: 14-SEP-12
It's on a Friday


BEGIN
  birthday('11-APR-81');
END;

Your next birthday is: 11-APR-13
It's on a Thursday
```

FUNCTIONS

A stored function has the same basic structure as a stored procedure. However, the heading of a function must include a RETURN clause. This clause specifies the data type of the value that the function returns. Functions must always return a value to the invoking process. The basic syntax to create a function is:

```
CREATE [OR REPLACE] FUNCTION function_name
       [(argument1  [mode1]   datatype1,
         Argument2  [mode2]   datatype2,
         …)]
RETURN datatype
IS|AS
BEGIN
  function_body;
END [function_name];
```

To demonstrate the difference between procedures and functions, the BIRTHDAY procedure is dropped and replace by a function. Two RETURN clauses are added, one in the heading and a second in the executable section of the function. Instead of using DBMS_OUTPUT to return the information, the text is returned by the function. The function is then called in three different fashions: via a SQL statement, in a PL/SQL block, and using EXECUTE to populate a host variable.

```
CREATE OR REPLACE FUNCTION birthday(p_birthdate   DATE)
RETURN VARCHAR2
IS
   v_next_bday     DATE;
   v_retval        VARCHAR2(80);
BEGIN
   v_next_bday := TO_DATE(TO_CHAR(p_birthdate, 'DD-MON') ||
                          TO_CHAR(SYSDATE, 'YY'));

   IF v_next_bday < SYSDATE THEN
     v_next_bday := ADD_MONTHS(v_next_bday, 12);
   END IF;

   v_retval := 'Your next birthday is: ' ||
               TO_CHAR(v_next_bday, 'DD-MON-YY') || '. ' ||
               'It''s on a ' ||
               TO_CHAR(v_next_bday, 'Day');

   RETURN v_retval;
END;
```

```
SELECT birthday('22-MAY-76')
FROM    dual;

BIRTHDAY('22-MAY-76')
-----------------------------------------------------------
Your next birthday is: 22-MAY-13. It's on a Wednesday


DECLARE
  v_birthtext    VARCHAR2(80);
BEGIN
  v_birthtext := birthday('12-NOV-91');
  DBMS_OUTPUT.PUT_LINE(v_birthtext);
END;

Your next birthday is: 12-NOV-12. It's on a Monday



VARIABLE  h_birthtext VARCHAR2(80)

EXECUTE :h_birthtext := birthday('02-AUG-88')

PRINT h_birthtext

H_BIRTHTEXT
-----------------------------------------------------------
Your next birthday is: 02-AUG-12. It's on a Thursday
```

PARAMETERS

For procedures or functions that contain parameters, they are declared after the subprogram name and before the IS keyword. There will always be two classes of parameters, which are defined as follows:

- **Formal parameters** -- Formal parameters are declared in the subprogram heading. For each formal parameter declaration, the name and data type of the parameter is specified, and (optionally) its mode and default value. Formal parameters can be referenced in the execution part of the subprogram by their declared names.

- **Actual Parameters** -- The actual parameters are specified when invoking the subprogram. These determine the values that are to be assigned to the formal parameters.

The mode of a formal parameter determines its behavior. There are three modes for formal parameters in PL/SQL and the mode used determines the direction in which information is passed via the parameter:

- **IN** -- This is the default parameter mode and need not be explicitly specified. It is used to pass a value to the subprogram.
- **OUT** -- OUT variables must be specified in the declaration of the subprogram and are used to return a value to the invoker.
- **IN OUT** -- IN OUT variables must be specified in the declaration of the subprogram and are used to pass an initial value to the subprogram and return an updated value to the invoker.

PACKAGES

PL/SQL packages are schema objects that allow you to group multiple procedures and functions along with any associated types, global constants, variables, cursors, and exceptions. As with named procedures and functions, packages are stored in the database in compiled form. Packages are defined in two parts, the specification and the body.

- **Package Specification** -- The specification declares public items that can be referenced from outside the package. Package specifications that do not contain cursors or subprograms can exist independently. Package specs with either of these must have an associated package body.
- **Package Body** – The body defines the code of public subprograms and the queries of public cursors. The package body can also declare and define private items that cannot be referenced from outside the package (such as variables, constants, types, and

cursors). The body can also contain initialization information that declares global variables and an exception-handling part.

The syntax for creating a package specification is:

```
CREATE [OR REPLACE] PACKAGE package_name
IS | AS
    public type and variable declarations
    subprogram specifications
END [package_name];
```

Any types, variables, constants or subprograms declared in the package specification are public. These are visible outside the package and can be invoked by other PL/SQL constructs. To make a procedure or function public within a package, declare the procedure or function header in the specification. Procedures and functions in a package being invoked by external constructs must use the package name as a prefix. Any public variables, types or constants referenced externally must likewise be prefixed. It a package specification contains no subprogram declarations or cursors then a package body is not required.

The syntax for creating a package body is:

```
CREATE [OR REPLACE] PACKAGE BODY package_name
IS | AS
    private type and variable declarations
    subprogram bodies
END [package_name];
```

The body of a package has a header, declaration, and an optional executable section. The executable section of a package body must be after all subprograms are declared. It is specified using the BEGIN keyword and ends with the END package_name line. Any code in this section is executed the first time the package is referenced within a session. The code will not be executed again unless the user changes sessions or the package is recompiled.

Packages, unlike procedures and functions, cannot be called, parameterized, or nested. Any types, variables or constants declared in the package body are private. They are only visible from inside the package. Likewise any subprograms that exist in the package body but are not declared in the package specification are private and can only be referenced from inside the package.

PL/SQL Programming Concepts: Review

List restrictions on calling functions from SQL expressions

There are numerous restrictions on what is possible when calling functions from a SQL statement. The following conditions must all be met:

- When invoked from a SELECT statement or a parallelized INSERT, UPDATE, or DELETE statement, the function cannot modify any database tables.
- When invoked from an INSERT, UPDATE, or DELETE statement, the function cannot query or modify any database tables modified by that statement.
- The function may not end a transaction via ROLLBACK or COMMIT or call a subprogram that does.
- It may contain only IN mode parameters with valid SQL data types.
- It must return valid SQL data types, not PL/SQL specific data types.
- The schema issuing the SQL must have EXECUTE privileges on the function.
- Parameters can only be passed using positional notation.

Handle exceptions

Exceptions are PL/SQL run-time errors and can be raised implicitly by Oracle or explicitly by the code in a PL/SQL block. The EXCEPTION section of a PL/SQL block is used for the purpose of trapping exceptions and handling them before they are passed to the calling environment. If a runtime error occurs in a PL/SQL block, and there is no EXCEPTION clause in scope to take action on the error, then the result is an unhandled exception. Exceptions are either trapped or propagated:

- **Trapped Exceptions** – If an exception occurs in a block that contains an EXCEPTION section, and that section contains the logic to handle the exception that was raised, then the exception is trapped and the block completes normally. The exception is not propagated to enclosing blocks, calling subprograms, or the host environment.

- **Propagated Exceptions** – If the block where an exception occurs does not have an EXCEPTION section, or the section does not have the logic to trap the exception that was raised, then the block terminates abnormally and the exception is propagated. If the subprogram was nested, the exception will be passed to the parent block. If the block was not nested, but it was called from another subprogram, then exception will propagate to the calling block. The exception will propagate back along the chain to where a PL/SQL subprogram was initially invoked from the host environment. If the exception is not handled by then, an unhandled exception is passed to the calling environment. At any point while the exception is propagating through PL/SQL blocks, it can be trapped by an exception section.

The example below shows the result of an unhandled exception:

```
DECLARE
   v_empid    NUMBER;
BEGIN
   SELECT employee_id
   INTO   v_empid
   FROM   hr.employees;
END;

Error report:
ORA-01422: exact fetch returns more than requested number of
rows
ORA-06512: at line 4
01422. 00000 -  "exact fetch returns more than requested
number of rows"
*Cause:    The number specified in exact fetch is less than
the rows returned.
```

```
*Action:    Rewrite the query or change number of rows
requested
```

Pre-defined exceptions

There are a number of exceptions that have names declared globally in the package STANDARD. For these errors, the system raises the exceptions implicitly at runtime. Because they have names, it is possible to create exception handlers for them. The below example adds an EXCEPTION clause to the previous one that handles the ORA-01422 error encountered. ORA-1422 has the redefined name TOO_MANY_ROWS.

```
DECLARE
  v_empid    NUMBER;
BEGIN
  SELECT employee_id
  INTO   v_empid
  FROM   hr.employees;

EXCEPTION
  WHEN TOO_MANY_ROWS THEN
     DBMS_OUTPUT.PUT_LINE('Too many rows returned by query');
END;

Too many rows returned by query
```

A partial list of other predefined exceptions is:

- **CASE_NOT_FOUND** -- ORA-06592
- **CURSOR_ALREADY_OPEN** -- ORA-06511
- **INVALID_NUMBER** -- ORA-01722
- **NO_DATA_FOUND** -- ORA-00100
- **ROWTYPE_MISMATCH** -- ORA-06504
- **VALUE_ERROR** -- ORA-06502

Non-predefined exceptions

Oracle has hundreds of internally defined exceptions (ORA-xxxxx errors). Only a tiny fraction of the internally defined exceptions are also predefined exceptions. An internally defined exception is an error condition in the database that Oracle has defined that will be raised when certain conditions are met. A predefined exception is a descriptive name assigned to an internally defined exception. For example: "ORA-01422" is an internally defined exception. "TOO_MANY_ROWS" is the predefined exception assigned to ORA-01422.

If there is no name defined for an exception, you can only handle it using a 'WHEN OTHERS' condition. To associate a name with an internally defined exception, you must do the following:

1. Declare the name in the declarative part of the appropriate block. An exception name declaration has the syntax:

    ```
    exception_name EXCEPTION;
    ```
2. Associate the declared name with the appropriate code for the internally defined exception. The syntax is:

    ```
    PRAGMA EXCEPTION_INIT (exception_name, error_code)
    ```

The following example gives the name X_SNAPSHOT_TOO_OLD to the internally defined exception ORA-01555 (Snapshot too old):

```
DECLARE
  x_snapshot_too_old    EXCEPTION;
  PRAGMA EXCEPTION_INIT(x_snapshot_too_old, -1555);
BEGIN
...
EXCEPTION
  WHEN x_snapshot_too_old THEN
...
END;
```

Unexpected internally-defined errors must be trapped through the use of the OTHERS clause. When using this, you can grab the specific error number and message. The following example makes use of WHEN OTHERS to trap exceptions and outputs the name and error message encountered:

```
DECLARE
  v_empid   NUMBER;
BEGIN
  SELECT employee_id
  INTO   v_empid
  FROM   hr.employees;

EXCEPTION
  WHEN OTHERS THEN
    DBMS_OUTPUT.PUT_LINE('SQLCODE: ' || SQLCODE);
    DBMS_OUTPUT.PUT_LINE('SQLERRM: ' || SQLERRM);
END;

SQLCODE: -1422
SQLERRM: ORA-01422: exact fetch returns more than requested
number of rows
```

User-defined exceptions

User-defined exceptions are for creating and handling exceptions that are related to your own application or business logic. They are not Oracle errors, so the runtime system will not be able to recognize when they occur. They must be raised explicitly. It is possible to do this with either the RAISE statement or RAISE_APPLICATION_ERROR procedure. When RAISE is called from outside an exception handler, the exception name to be raised must be specified. When called from inside an exception handler, issuing a RAISE with no exception name will re-raise the current exception. Exceptions can be declared in the declarative part of any PL/SQL anonymous block, subprogram, or package. The declaration has the following syntax:

```
exception_name EXCEPTION;
```

In the example below, the procedure declares an exception named x_weekend_date. When a supplied date evaluates to either Saturday or Sunday, the procedure raises the exception explicitly, and handles it with an exception handler.

```
CREATE OR REPLACE PROCEDURE submit_timesheet (p_ts_date DATE)
IS
   x_weekend_date EXCEPTION;
BEGIN
   IF TO_CHAR(p_ts_date, 'DY') IN ('SAT', 'SUN') THEN
      RAISE x_weekend_date;
   END IF;

EXCEPTION
   WHEN x_weekend_date THEN
      DBMS_OUTPUT.PUT_LINE ('Cannot submit timesheet for weekend dates.');
END;

BEGIN
   submit_timesheet ('17-JUN-12');
END;

Cannot submit timesheet for weekend dates.
```

RAISE_APPLICATION_ERROR

The RAISE_APPLICATION_ERROR procedure is part of the DBMS_STANDARD package and can be invoked only from a stored subprogram or method. It is normally used to raise a user-defined exception and return the error code and message to the invoker. Prior to calling RAISE_APPLICATION_ERROR, you must have assigned an error code to the exception using the EXCEPTION_INIT pragma:

```
PRAGMA EXCEPTION_INIT (exception_name, error_code)
```

RAISE_APPLICATION_ERROR is invoked using the following syntax:

```
RAISE_APPLICATION_ERROR (error_code, message[, {TRUE |
FALSE}]);
```

The error_code must be an integer in the range -20000..-20999. The message returned must be a character string of no more than 2048 bytes. When TRUE is specified, PL/SQL puts error_code on top of the error stack. If you specify false or leave it blank, PL/SQL replaces the error stack with error_code.

Manage dependencies

Procedures and functions sometimes have dependencies on other objects built into their definition. When stored subprograms include SQL statements against tables or views, invoke other stored subprograms, or generate values from a sequence, then they are said to reference those objects.

- **Dependent Object** -- Any object in the database that references one or more other objects as part of its definition is a dependent object.
- **Referenced Object** -- Any object that is referenced in the definition of another database object is referred to as a referenced object.

A subprogram may either directly or indirectly reference a table, view, procedure, function, sequence, or packaged functions, procedures, types, etc.

- **Direct Dependency** – Object A references Object B. Object A has a direct dependency on Object B.
- **Indirect Dependency** -- Object A references Object B. Object B references Object C. Object A has a direct dependency on Object B and an indirect dependency on Object C.

For example, a procedure or function with a direct dependency on a view has an indirect dependency on any tables in the view's definition. Likewise a subprogram with a direct dependency on a procedure is indirectly dependent on any objects that procedure references. A change to the objects that are indirectly dependent can cause the direct dependent to become invalid, and therefore the subprogram itself will become invalid. This is cascading invalidation.

If an object is not valid when it is referenced, it must be validated before being used. Validation occurs automatically when an object is referenced. When an object is invalidated, on the next access, the compiler will attempt to recompile. If it recompiles without errors, it is revalidated; otherwise, it will remain invalid. When the definition of a referenced object is changed, this may prevent dependent objects from being able to recompile. For example, if a table is dropped, then any view that queries that table can no longer function. Any procedure referencing that view will be unable to compile successfully.

The USER_DEPENDENCIES can be queried to display all the direct dependencies on an object in your schema. The dependent objects in this table will be only ones in your schema, but the referenced objects can be in any schema. The ALL_DEPENDENCIES and DBA_DEPENDENCIES views display the same information for all dependent objects to which you have access, and all dependent objects in the database respectively. Each has an OWNER column to reference the owner of the object. None of these views will display indirect dependencies. The following two queries display information about the dependencies that the OCPGURU schema has on the HR schema:

```
SELECT  name, referenced_name, referenced_type
FROM    user_dependencies
WHERE   type = 'PROCEDURE'
AND     referenced_owner = 'HR'

NAME              REFERENCED_NAME  REFERENCED_TYPE
----------------  ---------------  ---------------
GET_EMPLOYEE      EMPLOYEES        TABLE
EMP_YEARS         EMPLOYEES        TABLE
EMPS_DS           EMPLOYEES        TABLE
```

```
SELECT DISTINCT type, referenced_name, referenced_type
FROM     user_dependencies
WHERE    referenced_owner = 'HR'

TYPE             REFERENCED_NAME      REFERENCED_TYPE
-------------    -----------------    ---------------
SYNONYM          DEPARTMENTS          TABLE
PACKAGE BODY     EMPLOYEES            TABLE
PROCEDURE        EMPLOYEES            TABLE
```

To find all of the indirect dependencies using these views, you would have to query the dependencies of referenced objects shown, and then any they reference, and so on. The UTLDTREE.SQL script file creates two additional views (DEPTREE and IDEPTREE), and a procedure (DEPTREE_FILL). These can be used to provide a much easier means for finding indirect dependencies. Once this script file has been run in your schema, you can execute the DEPTREE_FILL procedure against an object that might be referenced by one or more objects (either directly or indirectly). The procedure will locate all objects that have a dependency on the identified object. The results can be viewed in by querying the DEPTREE or IDEPTREE views created by the script. The syntax to run the DEPTREE_FILL procedure is:

```
EXECUTE deptree_fill ('object_type', 'object_owner',
'object_name')
```

The two views created by the UTLDTREE.SQL script are used to display the direct and indirect dependencies on a given object. This can help you to determine what objects in the database might be invalidated if you make changes to a particular object. If one or more objects might be invalidated, you might decide not to alter the object, or to alter it after hours, or simply to recompile those objects explicitly after changing the referenced object.

The example below creates a function and a procedure that references it. The DIRECT_REFERENCE function references the view

EMPLOYEES_DEPT_V. The procedure DEPENDDENT_PROC calls the function (and therefore references it). The procedure then has a direct dependency on the function, and an indirect dependency on the view. The results from the queries against DEPTREE and IDEPTREE show this (as expected):

```
CREATE FUNCTION direct_reference
RETURN VARCHAR2
AS
  v_retval    VARCHAR2(20);
BEGIN
  SELECT last_name
  INTO   v_retval
  FROM   employees_dept_v
  WHERE  employee_id = 116;

  RETURN v_retval;
END direct_reference;

CREATE PROCEDURE dependent_proc
AS
  v_retval    VARCHAR2(20);
BEGIN
  v_retval := direct_reference;
END dependent_proc;


EXECUTE deptree_fill('VIEW', 'OCPGURU', 'EMPLOYEES_DEPT_V');
anonymous block completed


SELECT * FROM deptree;

NESTED_LEVEL TYPE        SCHEMA     NAME                       SEQ#
------------ ----------- ---------- -------------------------- ----
           1 FUNCTION    OCPGURU    DIRECT_REFERENCE              2
           2 PROCEDURE   OCPGURU    DEPENDENT_PROC                3
           0 VIEW        OCPGURU    EMPLOYEES_DEPT_V              0
```

```
SELECT * FROM ideptree;

DEPENDENCIES
-----------------------------------
FUNCTION OCPGURU.DIRECT_REFERENCE
PROCEDURE OCPGURU.DEPENDENT_PROC
VIEW OCPGURU.EMPLOYEES_DEPT_V
```

Use Oracle-supplied packages

A number of utilities are included with the Oracle database in the form of packages. These packages provide a significant level of functionality to the database that would otherwise require a great deal of coding to effect. A complete list of the Oracle-supplied packages can be obtained from the PL/SQL Packages and Types Reference manual. A partial list includes the following:

- **DBMS_ALERT** -- Provides support for the asynchronous notification of database events
- **DBMS_CRYPTO** -- Lets you encrypt and decrypt stored data.
- **DBMS_DATAPUMP** -- Lets you move all, or part of, a database between databases, including both data and metadata.
- **DBMS_LOCK** -- Lets you request, convert and release locks through Oracle Lock Management services
- **DBMS_OUTPUT** -- Accumulates information in a buffer so that it can be retrieved later
- **DBMS_PIPE** -- Provides a service which enables messages to be sent between sessions
- **DBMS_UTILITY** -- Provides various utility routines
- **UTL_HTTP** -- Enables HTTP callouts from PL/SQL and SQL to access data on the Internet or to call Oracle Web Server Cartridges
- **UTL_TCP** -- Provides PL/SQL functionality to support simple TCP/IP-based communications between servers and the outside world

Three of the most commonly used packages are DBMS_OUTPUT, UTL_FILE, and UTL_MAIL:

DBMS_OUTPUT

The DBMS_OUTPUT package allows PL/SQL to display output for reporting or debugging purposes. In order for this command to display output in SQL*Plus, you must issue the command, SET SERVEROUTPUT ON.

The various procedures in DBMS_OUTPUT are:

- **DISABLE** -- Disables calls to PUT, PUT_LINE, NEW_LINE, GET_LINE, and GET_LINES. It also purges the buffer of any remaining information. There is no need to call this procedure when using the SERVEROUTPUT option of SQL*Plus. The syntax is:

```
DBMS_OUTPUT.DISABLE;
```

- **ENABLE** -- Enables calls to PUT, PUT_LINE, NEW_LINE, GET_LINE, and GET_LINES. If the DBMS_OUTPUT package is not activated then calls to these procedures are ignored. The syntax is:

```
DBMS_OUTPUT.ENABLE (buffer_size IN INTEGER DEFAULT
20000);
```

- **GET_LINE** -- Retrieves a single line of buffered information. The syntax is:

```
DBMS_OUTPUT.GET_LINE (line OUT VARCHAR2,
                     status OUT INTEGER);
```

- **GET_LINES** -- Retrieves an array of lines from the buffer. This procedure is overloaded and has two alternate calls:

```
DBMS_OUTPUT.GET_LINES (lines    OUT CHARARR,
                      numlines IN OUT INTEGER);

DBMS_OUTPUT.GET_LINES (lines    OUT
DBMSOUTPUT_LINESARRAY,
                      numlines IN OUT INTEGER);
```

- **NEW_LINE** -- Puts an end-of-line marker. The GET_LINE Procedure and the GET_LINES Procedure return "lines" as delimited by "newlines". Every call to the PUT_LINE Procedure or NEW_LINE Procedure generates a line that is returned by GET_LINE(S). The syntax is:

    ```
    DBMS_OUTPUT.NEW_LINE;
    ```

- **PUT** -- Places a partial line in the buffer. The syntax is:

    ```
    DBMS_OUTPUT.PUT (item IN VARCHAR2);
    ```

- **PUT_LINE** -- Places a full line in the buffer (i.e. text plus a 'newline' character). The syntax is:

    ```
    DBMS_OUTPUT.PUT_LINE (item IN VARCHAR2);
    ```

UTL_FILE

The UTL_FILE package provides PL/SQL programs the ability to read and write from operating system files. Its I/O capabilities are similar to standard operating system stream file I/O (OPEN, GET, PUT, CLOSE) capabilities. The files and directories that are accessible to the user through UTL_FILE are controlled by several factors. The preferred method of granting access to an operating system directory for UTL_FILE is via an Oracle directory object. Directory objects can be created for any directory accessible to the Oracle server. Read and write access on the directory objects (and therefore the OS directory) can then be granted to individual database users. In the past, accessible directories for the UTL_FILE functions were specified with the initialization parameter UTL_FILE_DIR. Granting access using this method is no longer recommended. There are a number of different procedures and functions in the UTL_FILE package.

Some of the more commonly used are:

- **FCLOSE** -- Closes a file
- **FCLOSE_ALL** -- Closes all open file handles
- **FCOPY** -- Copies a contiguous portion of a file to a newly created file
- **FFLUSH** -- Physically writes all pending output to a file
- **FGETATTR** -- Reads and returns the attributes of a disk file
- **FGETPOS** -- Returns the current relative offset position within a file, in bytes
- **FOPEN** -- Opens a file for input or output
- **FREMOVE** -- Deletes a disk file, assuming that you have sufficient privileges
- **FRENAME** -- Renames an existing file to a new name.
- **GET_LINE** -- Reads text from an open file
- **GET_RAW** -- Reads a RAW string value from a file and adjusts the file pointer ahead by the number of bytes read
- **IS_OPEN** --Determines if a file handle refers to an open file
- **NEW_LINE** -- Writes one or more operating system-specific line terminators to a file
- **PUT** -- Writes a string to a file
- **PUT_LINE** -- Writes a line to a file and appends an operating system-specific line terminator

UTL_MAIL

The UTL_MAIL package allows you to send email from within PL/SQL. The package includes commonly used email features, such as attachments, CC, and BCC. In order for UTL_MAIL to be utilized, the initialization parameter SMTP_OUT_SERVER must be specified. UTL_MAIL is not installed by default because of security considerations and the initialization parameter requirement. In order to use the UTL_MAIL package, the invoking user will need to have the connect privilege granted in the access control list for the network host to which he wants to connect.

To install UTL_MAIL, you must run two scripts:

```
$ORACLE_HOME/rdbms/admin/utlmail.sql
$ORACLE_HOME/rdbms/admin/prvtmail.plb
```

The UTL_MAIL package includes the following procedures:

- **SEND** -- Packages an email message into the appropriate format, locates SMTP information, and delivers the message to the SMTP server for forwarding to the recipients.
- **SEND_ATTACH_RAW** -- The SEND Procedure overloaded for RAW attachments.
- **SEND_ATTACH_VARCHAR2** -- The SEND Procedure overloaded for VARCHAR2 attachments.

Designing PL/SQL Code

Identify guidelines for cursor design

Cursors in PL/SQL act as pointers to a private SQL area that stores information about a specific SQL statement. The cursors defined in PL/SQL are session cursors that exist only in session memory. When the session ends, the cursors cease to exist. Cursor attributes allow you to get information about session cursors and can be referenced via procedural statements but not through SQL statements. There are two broad classes of session cursors:

- **Implicit cursor** -- Implicit cursors, also known as SQL cursors, are constructed and managed by PL/SQL. PL/SQL will automatically open an implicit cursor when a SELECT or DML statement is run from within a PL/SQL block. You can access the attributes of implicit cursors, but there is no means by which you can control them. The syntax of an implicit cursor attribute value is 'SQL' followed by the attribute name. For the attribute %FOUND, the syntax to access would be SQL%FOUND. The SQLattribute reference will always point to the most recently run SELECT or DML statement. If no statements have been run, the value of SQLattribute will be NULL.
- **Explicit cursor** -- Explicit cursors are constructed and managed by user-code. Explicit cursors are declared and defined in a block. They will have a name and be associated with a query. The rows returned by an explicit cursor can be processed by using the OPEN, FETCH and CLOSE statements. Alternately the cursor can be used in a cursor FOR LOOP statement. It is not possible to assign a value to an explicit cursor, use it in an expression, or use it as a formal subprogram parameter or host variable. Because an explicit cursor is named, it can be referenced by name and is sometimes referred to as a named cursor. The attributes of an explicit cursor are referenced by the cursor name followed by the attribute. For a cursor called c_emps, the %FOUND attribute could be accessed via c_emps%FOUND.

The following four attributes are available to both implicit and explicit cursors:

- **%ISOPEN** -- This attribute returns TRUE if the cursor is open and FALSE if not. For an implicit cursor, while this attribute is technically available, it will always return FALSE, because an implicit cursor closes once its associated statement runs.
- **%FOUND** -- This attribute will return NULL, TRUE or FALSE :
    - ✓ NULL: Implicit cursors will return NULL if no SELECT or DML statement has run in the session. For explicit cursors it will return NULL after the cursor has been defined but before the first FETCH occurs.
    - ✓ TRUE: If a SELECT statement returned one or more rows or a DML statement affected one or more rows.
    - ✓ FALSE: If a SQL statement ran but no rows were affected or returned.
- **%NOTFOUND** -- This is the logical opposite of the %FOUND attribute. It will return one of three values:
    - ✓ NULL: Implicit cursors will return NULL if no SELECT or DML statement has run in the session. For explicit cursors it will return NULL after the cursor has been defined but before the first FETCH occurs.
    - ✓ TRUE: If a SQL statement ran but no rows were affected or returned.
    - ✓ FALSE: if a SELECT statement returned one or more rows or a DML statement affected one or more rows.
- **%ROWCOUNT** -- The row count attribute indicates the number of rows that were affected by a SQL operation. It returns a NULL for implicit cursors if no SELECT or DML statement has run in the session. For explicit cursors it will return NULL after the cursor has been defined but before the first FETCH occurs. In all other cases, it will return the number of rows returned by a SELECT statement or affected by a DML statement.

Attribute Guidelines

Attributes are Transient -- The values accessible via cursor attributes will always be those of the most recently executed SQL statement. When executing multiple SQL statements, either within the same PL/SQL block or via calls to other blocks, it is easy to overwrite the attribute value you need before the point where the value is to be tested. Saving attribute values to a local variable immediately after executing the SQL may be necessary. In the following example, after the employees table is updated, a procedure queries the minimum salary of the employees in that department. Even though the SQL in the procedure is being run in a separate PL/SQL block, it will overwrite the SQLAttribute values and the v_count variable will not show the number of rows affected by the UPDATE statement.

```
DECLARE
   v_dept_id    NUMBER   := 60;
   v_count      NUMBER;
BEGIN
   UPDATE hr.employees
   SET    salary = salary + 100
   WHERE  department_id = v_dept_id
   AND    salary < 2500;

   get_min_salary(v_dept_id);
   v_count := SQL%FOUND;
END;
```

To be sure of getting the correct attribute value, you should access attributes immediately after the SQL in question. If the value is not required until later in the block, then assign the attribute to a local variable so it will be available when you need it.

```
DECLARE
  v_dept_id    NUMBER    := 60;
  v_count      NUMBER;
BEGIN
  UPDATE hr.employees
  SET     salary = salary + 100
  WHERE   department_id = v_dept_id
  AND     salary < 2500;
  v_count := SQL%FOUND;

  get_min_salary(v_dept_id);
END;
```

The %NOTFOUND attribute does not provide useful information when used with SELECT INTO. If a SELECT INTO statement returns no row, then a NO_DATA_FOUND exception is raised. This blocks the execution flow before the attribute can be checked. If SELECT INTO is used as part of an aggregate function (i.e. SELECT MAX(colname) INTO...), then the SQL statement will always return either a value or a NULL, so the %NOTFOUND attribute will always be false.

Explicit Cursor Guidelines

Explicit Cursors provide a greater degree of control over query processing than implicit cursors. They can be declared in the declarative part of any PL/SQL block, subprogram, or package. An explicit cursor can be declared first and then defined later in the same block, subprogram, or package, or declared and defined simultaneously.

The syntax for declaring an explicit cursor without defining it is:

```
CURSOR cursor_name [ parameter_list ] RETURN return_type;
```

If a cursor has been declared, then an explicit cursor definition defines it. If it has not been declared, the definition both declares and defines it. The syntax for an explicit cursor definition is:

```
CURSOR cursor_name [ parameter_list ] [ RETURN return_type ]
IS select_statement;
```

The following block shows several methods of declaring and defining explicit cursors:

```
DECLARE
  -- Declare c1 without defining it
  CURSOR c1 RETURN hr.regions%ROWTYPE;

  -- Declare and define c2
  CURSOR c2 IS
    SELECT employee_id, job_id, salary
    FROM   hr.employees
    WHERE  job_id = 'SA_MAN';

  -- Define c1
  CURSOR c1 RETURN hr.regions%ROWTYPE IS
    SELECT *
    FROM   hr.regions;

  v_region_rec    hr.regions%ROWTYPE;
  v_employee_id   hr.employees.employee_id%TYPE;
  v_job_id        hr.employees.job_id%TYPE;
  v_salary        hr.employees.salary%TYPE;
BEGIN
  OPEN c1;
  LOOP
    FETCH c1 INTO v_region_rec;
    EXIT WHEN c1%NOTFOUND;
    -- Row Processing
  END LOOP;
  CLOSE c1;

  OPEN c2;
  LOOP
    FETCH c2 INTO v_employee_id, v_job_id, v_salary
    EXIT WHEN c2%NOTFOUND;
    -- Row Processing
  END LOOP;
  CLOSE c2;
END;
```

In the example above, a single record variable was created to hold the values from the c1 cursor. For the c2 cursor, three individual variables were declared. Using a record variable reduces the coding required to define the cursor and makes the resulting block simpler to read.

When using explicit cursors, good coding practice is to close them explicitly once they are no longer required. Open cursors consume memory and can maintain row-level locks. Also, only a limited number of open cursors are allowed per session, so opening enough cursors without closing them can generate an exception.

Explicit cursors require more code than other techniques such as the SQL cursor FOR loop. Using them, however, provides greater flexibility. It is possible to process several queries in parallel by declaring and opening multiple cursors. It is also possible to process multiple rows in a single loop iteration, or to skip rows, or split the processing of a single cursor into multiple loops. That said, if you don't need this flexibility, then a cursor FOR loop is the simpler (and therefore better) option.

Explicit cursors can be created with parameters specified in the definition. The parameters can be used in the WHERE clause and make cursors more flexible and reduce duplication of code. The following example shows a parameter for the job_id field. The parameter is given a default value in the definition. When the cursor is opened without supplying a parameter value, the default is used.

```
DECLARE
  CURSOR c1 (p_job_id VARCHAR2 DEFAULT 'SA_MAN') RETURN
hr.employees%ROWTYPE IS
    SELECT *
    FROM   hr.employees
    WHERE  job_id = p_job_id;

  v_emp_rec    hr.employees%ROWTYPE;

BEGIN
  -- Open cursor with default parameter value
  OPEN c1;
  LOOP
    FETCH c1 INTO v_emp_rec;
    EXIT WHEN c1%NOTFOUND;
    -- Row Processing
  END LOOP;
  CLOSE c1;
```

```
  -- Open cursor and specify parameter value
  OPEN c1 ('PU_CLERK');
  LOOP
    FETCH c1 INTO v_emp_rec;
    EXIT WHEN c1%NOTFOUND;
    -- Row Processing
  END LOOP;
  CLOSE c1;
END;
```

The standard FETCH operation retrieves one row at a time. When fetching a large number of rows, there is an overhead involved that can result in poor performance. The BULK COLLECT clause will fetch all of the result rows at once into a collection and then allow you to process them from it. Used correctly, bulk operations can provide a significant reduction in the time required to process the query results. The following example demonstrates a bulk-fetch from a cursor into two collections and then displays the first nine rows from them.

```
DECLARE
  TYPE typ_empid IS TABLE OF hr.employees.employee_id%TYPE;
  TYPE typ_salary IS TABLE OF hr.employees.salary%TYPE;
  t_empid    typ_empid;
  t_salary   typ_salary;

  CURSOR c1 IS
    SELECT employee_id, salary
    FROM   hr.employees
    WHERE  job_id = 'ST_CLERK';
BEGIN
  OPEN c1;
  FETCH c1 BULK COLLECT INTO t_empid, t_salary;
  CLOSE c1;

  FOR v_Lp IN t_empid.FIRST .. t_empid.LAST LOOP
    IF v_Lp < 10 THEN
       DBMS_OUTPUT.PUT_LINE( t_empid(v_Lp) || ' -- ' ||
t_salary(v_Lp));
    END IF;
  END LOOP;
END;
```

```
125 -- 3200
126 -- 2700
127 -- 2400
128 -- 2200
129 -- 3300
130 -- 2800
131 -- 2500
132 -- 2100
133 -- 3300
```

Use cursor variables

Cursor variables (sometimes referred to as a REF CURSOR) are somewhat like explicit cursors, however the two are not interchangeable. It is not allowed to use one where the other is expected. A cursor variable is not a cursor, but rather is a pointer to a cursor. Before a cursor variable can be used, it must be made to point to a SQL work area, either by opening it or by assigning it to another open PL/SQL or host cursor variable. Some of the ways in which a cursor variable is not like an explicit cursor are:

- It is not limited to a single query.
- It is possible to assign a value to it.
- It can be used in an expression.
- It can be a subprogram parameter.
- It can be a host variable.
- It cannot accept parameters.

A cursor variable can be created by declaring a variable of type SYS_REFCURSOR or by defining a REF CURSOR type and then using that to declare a cursor variable. The return type of a cursor variable is always a record type. The basic syntax for defining a REF CURSOR type is:

```
TYPE type_name IS REF CURSOR [ RETURN return_type ]
```

Cursor variables come in two broad classes:

Weak Cursor Variables

- Are defined without a return type.
- The SYS_REFCURSOR type is weak. Any cursor variables defined using it are also weak.
- Can be associated with any query.
- More prone to errors.
- More flexible.
- The value of a weak cursor variable can be assigned to any other weak cursor variable.

Strong Cursor Variables

- Are defined with a return type.
- Can be associated only queries that return the specified type.
- Less prone to errors.
- Less flexible.
- Value can be assigned to a second strong cursor variable only if both cursor variables have the same TYPE (not just the same return type).

The following block provides examples of strong and weak cursor variable type definitions.

```
DECLARE
  -- Strong cursor variable type using %ROWTYPE
  TYPE cv_emprowtyp IS REF CURSOR RETURN employees%ROWTYPE;

  -- Strong cursor variable
  cv_emprow   cv_emprowtyp;


  -- Strong cursor variable type using a defined RECORD type
  TYPE rec_DeptColsTyp IS RECORD (
       depaertment_id hr.departments.department_id%TYPE,
       department_name
hr.departments.department_name%TYPE);

  TYPE cv_deptcolstyp IS REF CURSOR RETURN rec_DeptColsTyp;
  cv_deptcols cv_deptcolstyp;
```

```
   -- Weak cursor variable type
   TYPE cv_weaktyp IS REF CURSOR; -- weak type

   -- Weak cursor variable
   cv_generic cv_weaktyp;

   -- Weak cursor variable using SYS_REFCURSOR
   cv_refcur SYS_REFCURSOR;
BEGIN
   NULL;
END;
```

Once a cursor variable has been declared, it can be opened using the OPEN FOR statement. The OPEN FOR statement:

1. Associates a query to the cursor variable
2. Allocates database resources to the cursor variable
3. Executes the query
4. Places the cursor at the first row of the result set

At this point, the cursor variable acts much like an explicit cursor, with the FETCH command incrementally pulling in rows from the result set. The variable can be reused by another OPEN FOR statement without being closed. If OPEN FOR is executed against a query that is already open for a query, any information associated with the previous query is lost. Once processing is complete, close the cursor variable to release the resources.

When fetching the rows of the query result set, the cursor variable return type must be compatible with the INTO clause of the FETCH statement. For strong cursor variables, PL/SQL detects incompatibility at compile time. For weak cursor variables, PL/SQL detects incompatibility at run time, raising the ROWTYPE_MISMATCH exception. The following block creates a cursor variable, opens it, and loops through the query result set.

```
DECLARE
  cv_refcur SYS_REFCURSOR;

  v_employee_id    hr.employees.employee_id%TYPE;
  v_hire_date      hr.employees.hire_date%TYPE;
  v_salary         hr.employees.salary%TYPE;
BEGIN
  OPEN cv_refcur FOR
    SELECT employee_id, hire_date, salary
    FROM   hr.employees
    WHERE  job_id = 'IT_PROG'
    ORDER BY salary;

  LOOP
    FETCH cv_refcur
    INTO  v_employee_id, v_hire_date, v_salary;

    EXIT WHEN cv_refcur%NOTFOUND;

    DBMS_OUTPUT.PUT_LINE( v_employee_id || ': ' ||
                          TO_CHAR(v_hire_date, 'DD-MON-YY')
|| ' -- ' ||
                          v_salary );
  END LOOP;

  CLOSE cv_refcur;
END;
/

Result:
107: 07-FEB-07 -- 4200
105: 25-JUN-05 -- 4800
106: 05-FEB-06 -- 4800
104: 21-MAY-07 -- 6000
```

It is possible to assign the value of one cursor variable to another. The syntax is:

```
target_cursor_variable := source_cursor_variable;
```

If the source variable is open at the time of the assignment, then the target cursor variable will be open after the assignment and will point to the same SQL work area. If the source is not open at the time of the assignment, opening it afterward will not affect the target variable.

Cursor variables can be used as subprogram parameters. Used in this fashion, it is possible to pass query results between subprograms. If a cursor variable is declared as the formal parameter of a subprogram, the following rules apply:

- If the subprogram opens or assigns a value to the cursor variable, then the parameter mode must be IN OUT.
- If the subprogram only fetches from, or closes, the cursor variable, then the parameter mode can be either IN or IN OUT.
- Corresponding formal and actual cursor variable parameters must have compatible return types.

In order to pass a cursor variable parameter between subprograms in different PL/SQL units, a REF CURSOR type that matches the parameter should be declared in a package. Declaring a REF CURSOR type in a package allows multiple subprograms to use it to declare formal parameters and variables of that type. The following example declares a strong cursor variable in the package specification and then uses that cursor variable as a procedure parameter in the package body:

```
CREATE OR REPLACE PACKAGE cv_strong
AS

  TYPE cv_emprowtyp IS REF CURSOR
    RETURN hr.employees%ROWTYPE;

  PROCEDURE open_strong_cv (p_emp_cv IN OUT cv_emprowtyp,
                            p_flag   IN     PLS_INTEGER);
END cv_strong;
/

CREATE OR REPLACE PACKAGE BODY cv_strong
AS

PROCEDURE open_strong_cv (p_emp_cv IN OUT cv_emprowtyp,
                          p_flag   IN     PLS_INTEGER)
IS
BEGIN
  CASE p_flag
    WHEN 1 THEN
      OPEN p_emp_cv FOR SELECT *
                        FROM   hr.employees
                        WHERE  job_id = 'SA_MAN';
```

```
      WHEN 2 THEN
        OPEN p_emp_cv FOR SELECT *
                          FROM   hr.employees
                          WHERE  manager_id = 123;
      ELSE
        OPEN p_emp_cv FOR SELECT *
                          FROM   hr.employees
                          WHERE  department_id = 30;
    END CASE;
END open_strong_cv;
```

If the cursor variable had been declared without a without a return type, then, then it could be used for queries in the package that had more than one return type. The following example is similar to the above, but declares a weak cursor variable in the specification:

```
CREATE OR REPLACE PACKAGE cv_weak
AS

  TYPE cv_weakling IS REF CURSOR;

  PROCEDURE open_weak_cv (p_weak_cv IN OUT cv_weakling,
                          p_flag    IN     PLS_INTEGER);
END cv_weak;
/

CREATE OR REPLACE PACKAGE BODY cv_weak
AS

PROCEDURE open_weak_cv (p_weak_cv IN OUT cv_weakling,
                        p_flag    IN     PLS_INTEGER)
IS
BEGIN
  CASE p_flag
    WHEN 1 THEN
      OPEN p_weak_cv FOR SELECT *
                         FROM   hr.employees
                         WHERE  job_id = 'SA_MAN';
    WHEN 2 THEN
      OPEN p_weak_cv FOR SELECT *
                         FROM   hr.departments
                         WHERE  location_id = 1700;
    ELSE
      OPEN p_weak_cv FOR SELECT *
                         FROM   hr.regions;
  END CASE;
END open_weak_cv;
END cv_weak;
/
```

Create subtypes based on existing types

Subtypes are data types that are based on a scalar PL/SQL type -- whether it is a predefined type or a user-defined type. Subtypes can be either constrained or unconstrained.

- **Unconstrained** -- When a subtype is unconstrained, it contains the exact same set of values as the base type. Effectively it becomes an alias for the base type. Unconstrained subtypes are interchangeable with the base type or with other unconstrained subtypes on that base type. They are sometimes used to indicate the intended use of data items of that type.
- **Constrained** -- Constrained subtypes can accept only a subset of the values of its base type. They can be used to create types that are compatible with ANSI/ISO data types or to restrict values in the type to a set range.

The syntax to define an unconstrained subtype follows, where **subtype_name** is the name of the user-defined subtype being defined and **base_type** is the base type of the subtype being defined. The base_type must be scalar:

```
SUBTYPE subtype_name IS base_type
```

In the below example, the NUMBER TYPE is the base for creating three unconstrained subtypes, that show the intended uses of data items of their types (Mortgage Principal, Interest, and Escrow).

```
PROCEDURE mtg_pymt(p_payment  IN     NUMBER,
                   p_balance  IN OUT NUMBER)
IS
  SUBTYPE Principal IS NUMBER;
  SUBTYPE Interest  IS NUMBER;
  SUBTYPE Escrow    IS NUMBER;

  v_mort_princ      Principal(8,2);
  v_mort_int        Interest(8,2);
  v_mort_escrow     Escrow(8,2);

BEGIN
  v_mort_princ   := p_payment * .2;
```

```
   v_mort_int      := p_payment * .75;
   v_mort_escrow   := p_payment * .05;

   p_balance := p_balance - v_mort_princ;
END;
/
```

When a subtype is constrained, there is an additional restriction beyond that defined by the base type that restricts the subtype to a subset of data that can be held by the base type. The subtype can specify any attributes allowed by the base type (size, precision, scale, or a range of values). The syntax for declaring a constrained subtype is:

```
SUBTYPE subtype_name IS base_type
{ precision [, scale ] | RANGE low_value .. high_value } [
NOT NULL ]
```

If the base type does not allow size, precision, scale, or range restrictions, the only constraint that can added to any subtypes of it is NOT NULL:

```
SUBTYPE subtype_name IS base_type [ NOT NULL ]
```

In the following example a constrained subtype called Salary is set to detect and prevent out of range values. When a value out of the assigned range is assigned to a variable of this subtype, an exception occurs.

```
DECLARE
   SUBTYPE Salary IS NUMBER(8,2);

   v_emp_salary    Salary;
BEGIN
   v_emp_salary := 2000000.00;
END;
/

Error report:
ORA-06502: PL/SQL: numeric or value error: number precision
too large
ORA-06512: at line 6
06502. 00000 -  "PL/SQL: numeric or value error%s"
*Cause:
*Action:
```

The values in a variable of a constrained subtype can always be implicitly converted to the base type it was defined against. However, values in a variable of the base type can only be implicitly converted to a subtype of it when the value in the variable does not violate the subtype's constraints. The same is true of two constrained subtypes of the same base type.

```
DECLARE
  SUBTYPE One_to_ten     IS PLS_INTEGER RANGE 1..10;
  SUBTYPE Eleven_to_20   IS PLS_INTEGER RANGE 11..20;
  SUBTYPE One_to_20      IS PLS_INTEGER RANGE 1..20;

  v_1_to_10    One_to_ten := 3;
  v_11_to_20   Eleven_to_20 := 15;
  v_1_to_20    One_to_20;
BEGIN
  v_1_to_20 := v_1_to_10;   -- No error
  v_1_to_20 := v_11_to_20;  -- No error
  v_1_to_10 := v_11_to_20;  -- Out of range
END;
/

Error report:
ORA-06502: PL/SQL: numeric or value error
ORA-06512: at line 12
06502. 00000 -  "PL/SQL: numeric or value error%s"
*Cause:
*Action
```

Working with Collections

Create collections

Collections are one of two composite data types that can be defined in PL/SQL (the other composite type being a record). Unlike scalar data types, composite data types contain internal components that can be accessed individually. These internal components can themselves be either scalar or another composite data type (for example a collection might contain a record as an internal component). The internal components, composite or scalar, can be used any place that a variable of the same type can be used. The internal components of a collection are called elements, always have the same data type and are accessed via an index value. Elements in a collection are accessed via the following syntax:

```
variable_name(index)
```

It is possible to create a collection of records (or a record that contains collections). In records, the internal components can have different data types, and are called fields. Fields in a record variable are accessed with this syntax:

```
variable_name.field_name
```

There are three different types of collections available in PL/SQL. They each have different capabilities and uses. Much of their capabilities are determined by the following six attributes:

- **Number of Elements** -- For collections where the number of elements is specified, it is the maximum number of elements in the collection. For collection types where the number of elements is unspecified, the maximum number of elements in the collection is the upper limit of the index type.
- **Index Type** -- This is the data type(s) allowed for the value used to index collection elements.
- **Dense or Sparse** -- When a collection is dense, there are never gaps between elements. Every element between the first and last element is defined and has a value (which can be NULL). A sparse collection has gaps between elements.

- **Uninitialized Status** -- An empty collection exists but has no elements. The EXTEND method is used to add elements. A null collection does not exist and must be initialized. It is initialized either by making it empty or by assigning a non-NULL value to it.
- **Where Defined** -- Collections can be defined in a PL/SQL block as a local type, in a package specification as a public item, or defined at the schema level as a standalone type using the CREATE TYPE Statement.
- **Can Be ADT Attribute Data Type** -- To be an ADT attribute data type, a collection type must be a standalone collection type.

The three collection types and their attributes are:

- **Associative array** -- This collection is also known as an "index-by table". The number of elements is unspecified. The index data type can be either a string or a PLS_INTEGER. It can be either dense or sparse. The uninitialized status is empty. Associative arrays can only be defined in a PL/SQL block or package and so cannot be an ADT attribute type.
- **VARRAY** -- This collection is also known as a "variable-size array". The number of elements is specified, indexed by an integer and always dense. The uninitialized status of the collection is NULL. VARRAYs can be defined in a PL/SQL block or package or defined at the schema level. When defined at the schema level, they can be an ADT attribute data type.
- **Nested table** -- A nested table collection has an unspecified number of elements that are indexed by integer values. They will start dense but may become sparse if elements are deleted. The uninitialized status is NULL. Nested tables can be defined in a PL/SQL block or package or defined at the schema level. When defined at the schema level, they can be an ADT attribute data type.

Nested Tables

Nested tables store an unspecified number of elements in no particular order. Until initialized, a nested table variable is a null collection. It must be initialized, either by making it empty or by assigning a non-NULL value to it. When the values in a nested table are assigned to a PL/SQL nested table variable, the elements are indexed by consecutive integers starting with 1. The index values allow you to access the individual elements in the nested table variable. The indexes and order of the elements in a nested table are not fixed and may change as the table is stored and retrieved from the database. The syntax to access an individual element is:

`variable_name(index)`.

The following PL/SQL block defines a local nested table type. It then declares a variable of that type and a named procedure to print all of the nested table element values. The named procedure is called after initializing the variable, after changing the value of one element, and after using a constructor to the change the values of all elements. A constructor is a system-defined function that is used to identify where data should be placed. It 'constructs' the collection based on the values passed to it.

```
DECLARE
  TYPE typ_GroceryList IS TABLE OF VARCHAR2(20);

  -- nested table variable initialized with constructor:
  tab_list typ_GroceryList := typ_GroceryList('Apples', 'Bananas',
                                              'Cherries', 'Peaches');

  PROCEDURE print_cl (p_header VARCHAR2)
  IS
  BEGIN
    DBMS_OUTPUT.PUT_LINE(p_header);
    FOR v_Lp IN tab_list.FIRST .. tab_list.LAST LOOP
      DBMS_OUTPUT.PUT_LINE(v_Lp || ': ' || tab_list(v_Lp));
    END LOOP;
    DBMS_OUTPUT.PUT_LINE('----------');
  END;

BEGIN
  print_cl('Initial Nested Table:');

  -- Change a single value
```

```
  tab_list(2) := 'Butter';
  print_cl('After changing Index 2:');

   -- Change the entire table
  tab_list := typ_GroceryList('Potato Chips', 'Cola',
'Donuts');
  print_cl('After changing table:');
END;
/

Initial Nested Table:
1: Apples
2: Bananas
3: Cherries
4: Peaches
----------
After changing Index 2:
1: Apples
2: Butter
3: Cherries
4: Peaches
----------
After changing table:
1: Potato Chips
2: Cola
3: Donuts
----------
```

The following example creates a standalone nested table type to use in the procedure. The standalone procedure from the previous example is used, with an addition to handle a sparse array. The main block prints the initial nested table, then deletes an element and reprints it. After element three is deleted, the nested table is no longer dense because it has no value at index three.

```
CREATE OR REPLACE TYPE typ_GroceryList IS TABLE OF
VARCHAR2(20);
/
```

```
DECLARE
  -- nested table variable initialized with constructor:
  tab_list typ_GroceryList := typ_GroceryList('Apples',
                   'Bananas', 'Cherries', 'Peaches');

  PROCEDURE print_cl (p_header VARCHAR2)
  IS
  BEGIN
    DBMS_OUTPUT.PUT_LINE(p_header);
    FOR v_Lp IN tab_list.FIRST .. tab_list.LAST LOOP
      IF tab_list.EXISTS(v_Lp) THEN
        DBMS_OUTPUT.PUT_LINE(v_Lp || ': ' || tab_list(v_Lp));
      END IF;
    END LOOP;
    DBMS_OUTPUT.PUT_LINE('----------');
  END;

BEGIN
  print_cl('Initial Nested Table:');

  -- Change a single value
  tab_list.DELETE(3);
  print_cl('After deleting Index 3:');

END;
/

Initial Nested Table:
1: Apples
2: Bananas
3: Cherries
4: Peaches
----------
After deleting Index 3:
1: Apples
2: Bananas
4: Peaches
----------
```

VARRAYs

A variable-size array, or VARRAY, is given a maximum number of elements when defined. The VARRY can have a number of elements raging from zero to that defined maximum. The elements are indexed with integers starting with a lower bound of 1. The upper bound changes depending on the number of elements up to the defined maximum. Unlike a nested table, when a VARRAY is stored and retrieved from the database, its indexes and element order remain stable. A VARRAY variable must be initialized, either by making it empty or by assigning a non-NULL value to it. Until initialized, a variable array is a null collection. The syntax to access an element of a varray variable is:

```
variable_name(index).
```

The block below defines a local VARRAY type with a maximum of four elements. It declares a variable of that type and initializes it with a constructor. The header contains a procedure that prints the varray. The print procedure is invoked in the main portion of the block three times to show the initial values and the values after two sets of changes.

```
DECLARE
  TYPE typ_herbs IS VARRAY(4) OF VARCHAR2(15);

  -- varray variable initialized with constructor:
  tab_garden  typ_herbs := typ_herbs('Cilantro', 'Oregano',
                                     'Rosemary', 'Garlic');

  PROCEDURE print_cl (p_header VARCHAR2)
  IS
  BEGIN
    DBMS_OUTPUT.PUT_LINE(p_header);
    FOR v_Lp IN tab_garden.FIRST .. tab_garden.LAST LOOP
      DBMS_OUTPUT.PUT_LINE(v_Lp || ': ' || tab_garden(v_Lp));
    END LOOP;
    DBMS_OUTPUT.PUT_LINE('----------');
  END;

BEGIN
  print_cl('First Garden:');

  tab_garden(1) := 'Dill';   -- Change values of two elements
  tab_garden(4) := 'Onions';
  print_cl('Second Garden:');

  -- Invoke constructor to assign new values to varray:
  tab_garden := Herbs('Parsley', 'Sage', 'Rosemary',
'Thyme');
  print_cl('Third Garden:');
END;
/
```

```
First Garden:
1: Cilantro
2: Oregano
3: Rosemary
4: Garlic
----------
Second Garden:
1: Dill
2: Oregano
3: Rosemary
4: Onions
----------
Third Garden:
1: Parsley
2: Sage
3: Rosemary
4: Thyme
----------
```

Associative Arrays

An associative array is a set of key-value pairs. They are sometimes referred to as a PL/SQL table or index-by table. The keys act as a unique index that can be used to access the associated value in the associative array. Keys can be either a PLS_INTEGER or a string type. When adding elements to the array, the indexes are stored in a sorted order rather than the order they were entered into the array. When the index is a string type, NLS_SORT and NLS_COMP determine the sort order. The information in an associative array is temporary. They are always pure-memory objects, never part of a database table. It is possible to make the data persistent in memory for the life of a database session by declaring the associative array in a package specification and populating it in the package body. Values in an associative array can be accessed with the syntax:

```
variable_name(index).
```

Some of the attributes of an associative array are:

- Arrays are empty, but not null, until they are populated
- Arrays can hold an unspecified number of elements, which can be accessed without knowing their positions
- Arrays do not require disk space or network operations
- Arrays cannot be manipulated with DML statements

The following block defines a type of associative array indexed by a VARCHAR2. It declares an associative array variable, populates it with five elements and prints the values. The values are printed in sorted order rather than the order they were created.

```
DECLARE
  TYPE typ_palette IS TABLE OF VARCHAR2(10)
    INDEX BY VARCHAR2(10);

  -- Declare an associative array variable
  tab_colors    typ_palette;

  v_index       VARCHAR2(10);
BEGIN
  -- Add elements (key-value pairs) to associative array:
  tab_colors('FF0000') := 'Red';
  tab_colors('0000FF') := 'Blue';
  tab_colors('00FFFF') := 'Cyan';
  tab_colors('00FF00') := 'Green';
  tab_colors('FF00FF') := 'Magenta';

  -- Print associative array:
  v_index := tab_colors.FIRST; -- Get first element of array
  WHILE v_index IS NOT NULL LOOP
    DBMS_OUTPUT.PUT_LINE('The color for ' || v_index ||
                         ' is ' || tab_colors(v_index));

    -- Get the next element
    v_index := tab_colors.NEXT(v_index);
  END LOOP;
END;
/

The color for 0000FF is Blue
The color for 00FF00 is Green
The color for 00FFFF is Cyan
The color for FF0000 is Red
The color for FF00FF is Magenta
```

Use collection methods

PL/SQL includes a set of procedures and functions called collection methods that return information about collections. The functionality provided by these methods makes collections easier to use. The basic syntax to invoke a collection method is:

```
collection_name.method
```

The available collection methods are:

- **DELETE** -- Deletes elements from the collection.
- **TRIM** -- Deletes elements from the end of a varray or nested table.
- **EXTEND** -- Adds elements to the end of a varray or nested table.
- **EXISTS** -- Returns TRUE if the specified element of varray or nested table exists. This is the only method that can be used against a null collection without raising the predefined exception COLLECTION_IS_NULL.
- **FIRST** -- Returns the first index in the collection.
- **LAST** -- Returns the last index in the collection.
- **COUNT** -- Returns number of elements in the collection.
- **LIMIT** -- Returns then maximum number of elements that the given collection can have.
- **PRIOR** -- Returns index that precedes the specified index.
- **NEXT** -- Returns index that succeeds the specified index

The following block demonstrates all of the collection methods except TRIM, EXTEND, and LIMIT – none of which are appropriate to an associative array.

```
DECLARE
  -- Associative array indexed by PLS_INTEGER:
  TYPE typ_numbers IS TABLE OF VARCHAR2(10)
    INDEX BY PLS_INTEGER;

  -- Declare an associative array variable
  tab_numbers    typ_numbers;

  v_index        PLS_INTEGER;
BEGIN
```

```
   IF tab_numbers.EXISTS(1) THEN
     DBMS_OUTPUT.PUT_LINE('Element 1 exists');
   ELSE
     DBMS_OUTPUT.PUT_LINE('Element 1 does not exist');
   END IF;

   -- Add elements (key-value pairs) to associative array:
   tab_numbers(1) := 'One';
   tab_numbers(2) := 'Two';
   tab_numbers(3) := 'Three';
   tab_numbers(4) := 'Four';
   tab_numbers(5) := 'Five';
   tab_numbers(6) := 'Six';
   tab_numbers(7) := 'Seven';
   tab_numbers(8) := 'Eight';
   tab_numbers(9) := 'Nine';
   tab_numbers(10) := 'Ten';

   IF tab_numbers.EXISTS(1) THEN
     DBMS_OUTPUT.PUT_LINE('Element 1 exists now');
   ELSE
     DBMS_OUTPUT.PUT_LINE('Element 1 still does not exist');
   END IF;
   DBMS_OUTPUT.PUT_LINE('---------------------------');

   -- Print FIRST element:
   v_index := tab_numbers.FIRST;
   DBMS_OUTPUT.PUT_LINE('The FIRST element is ' || tab_numbers(v_index));

   -- Print LAST element:
   v_index := tab_numbers.LAST;
   DBMS_OUTPUT.PUT_LINE('The LAST element is ' || tab_numbers(v_index));

   -- Print COUNT of elements:
   v_index := tab_numbers.COUNT;
   DBMS_OUTPUT.PUT_LINE('There are ' || v_index || ' elements.');
   DBMS_OUTPUT.PUT_LINE('---------------------------');

   -- Print NEXT element after 5:
   v_index := tab_numbers.NEXT(5);
   DBMS_OUTPUT.PUT_LINE('The element after index 5 is ' || tab_numbers(v_index));

   -- Print element PRIOR to 8:
   v_index := tab_numbers.PRIOR(8);
   DBMS_OUTPUT.PUT_LINE('The element before index 8 is ' || tab_numbers(v_index));
   DBMS_OUTPUT.PUT_LINE('---------------------------');
```

```
    -- DELETE element 3
    tab_numbers.DELETE(3);
    DBMS_OUTPUT.PUT_LINE('Deleted element 3');
    v_index := tab_numbers.PRIOR(4);
    DBMS_OUTPUT.PUT_LINE('The element before index 4 is ' ||
tab_numbers(v_index));

    -- DELETE all Elements
    tab_numbers.DELETE;
    DBMS_OUTPUT.PUT_LINE('Deleted all elements.');
    v_index := tab_numbers.COUNT;
    DBMS_OUTPUT.PUT_LINE('There are ' || v_index || '
elements.');

END;
/

Element 1 does not exist
Element 1 exists now
-------------------------
The FIRST element is One
The LAST element is Ten
There are 10 elements.
-------------------------
The element after index 5 is Six
The element before index 8 is Seven
-------------------------
Deleted element 3
The element before index 4 is Two
Deleted all elements.
There are 0 elements.
```

The following example uses a VARRAY to demonstrate the TRIM, EXTEND, and LIMIT methods:

```
DECLARE
  TYPE typ_numbers IS VARRAY(5) OF VARCHAR2(15);

  -- varray variable initialized with constructor:
  tab_numbers  typ_numbers := typ_numbers('One', 'Two',
'Three', 'Four');

  v_index       PLS_INTEGER;

  PROCEDURE print_cl (p_header VARCHAR2)
  IS
  BEGIN
    DBMS_OUTPUT.PUT_LINE(p_header);
    FOR v_Lp IN tab_numbers.FIRST .. tab_numbers.LAST LOOP
```

```
           DBMS_OUTPUT.PUT_LINE(v_Lp || ': ' ||
tab_numbers(v_Lp));
      END LOOP;
      DBMS_OUTPUT.PUT_LINE('----------');
   END;

BEGIN
   -- Print LIMIT of elements:
   v_index := tab_numbers.LIMIT;
   DBMS_OUTPUT.PUT_LINE('There is a LIMIT of ' || v_index || '
elements.');
   DBMS_OUTPUT.PUT_LINE('---------------------------');

   print_cl('Initial Values:');

   -- EXTEND VARRY by one:
   tab_numbers.EXTEND(1);
   tab_numbers(5) := 'Five';
   print_cl('Values after EXTEND:');

   -- TRIM VARRY by one:
   tab_numbers.TRIM(1);
   print_cl('Values after TRIM:');

END;
/

There is a LIMIT of 5 elements.
---------------------------
Initial Values:
1: One
2: Two
3: Three
4: Four
----------
Values after EXTEND:
1: One
2: Two
3: Three
4: Four
5: Five
----------
Values after TRIM:
1: One
2: Two
3: Three
4: Four
----------
```

Manipulate collections

The method required for manipulating the data in a collection varies considerably depending on which collection type is used. A significant feature is the ability of a PL/SQL procedure to use SQL to manipulate in-memory collections. With Nested tables and VARRAYs, it is possible to manipulate the data in a collection via SQL. With an associative array, the data can only be manipulated via PL/SQL calls.

Manipulating data in Nested Tables

To create a nested table, you might begin by defining an appropriate object type:

```
CREATE TYPE cert_test AS OBJECT (
        test_id      VARCHAR2(10),
        test_name    VARCHAR2(80),
        questions    NUMBER,
        time_mins    NUMBER);
```

The cert_test TYPE can then be incorporated into a TABLE type and the new TABLE type included as a column in a database table:

```
CREATE TYPE tbl_tests AS TABLE OF cert_test;

CREATE TABLE oracle_certifications (
        product_line    VARCHAR2(30),
        product_area    VARCHAR2(80),
        testing_area    VARCHAR2(80),
        exams           tbl_tests)
     NESTED TABLE exams STORE AS tests_tab;
```

The EXAMS column in the base table will store all of the exams for a given product line, product area, and testing area. The NESTED TABLE clause identifies the nested table and names the system-generated store table. The following exampled populates the ORACLE_CERTIFICATIONS table using the table constructor tbl_tests():

```
BEGIN
   INSERT INTO oracle_certifications
      VALUES('Database', 'Database Application Development',
      'SQL and PL/SQL',
      tbl_tests(cert_test('1Z0-047',
                          'Oracle Database SQL Expert',
                           70, 120),
                cert_test('1Z0-051',
                          'Oracle 11g: SQL Fundamentals I',
                           70, 120),
                cert_test('1Z0-144',
                          'Oracle 11g: Program with PL/SQL',
                           80, 90),
                cert_test('1Z0-146',
                          'Oracle 11g: Advanced PL/SQL',
                           68, 90),
                cert_test('1Z0-147',
                          'Program with PL/SQL',
                           66, 90)));
   INSERT INTO oracle_certifications
      VALUES('Database', 'Database Application Development',
      'Oracle Application Express (Oracle APEX)',
      tbl_tests(cert_test('1Z0-450',
                          'Oracle Apex 4: Dev. Web Apps',
                           55, 90)));
   INSERT INTO oracle_certifications
      VALUES('Database', 'Database Application Development',
      'MySQL Developer',
      tbl_tests(cert_test('1Z0-872',
                          'MySQL 5 Dev CP Exam, Part I',
                           70, 90),
                cert_test('1Z0-871',
                          'MySQL 5 Dev CP Exam, Part II',
                           70, 90)));
END;
```

The test numbers for 1Z0-871 and 1Z0-872 are reversed in the above example. To repair this, we can create a variable of the tbl_tests TYPE and define it with the correct data. A SQL statement can then be used to apply it to the base table. The code in the following block fixes the faulty data:

```
DECLARE
   v_fix tbl_tests :=
      tbl_tests(cert_test('1Z0-871',
                'MySQL 5 Dev CP Exam, Part I',
                 70, 90),
              cert_test('1Z0-872',
                'MySQL 5 Dev CP Exam, Part II',
                 70, 90));
BEGIN
   UPDATE oracle_certifications
   SET    exams = v_fix
   WHERE  testing_area = 'MySQL Developer';
END;
```

Manipulating data in VARRAYs

In SQL*Plus, suppose you define object type Answers, as follows:

```
CREATE TYPE Answers AS OBJECT (
           answer_id      VARCHAR2(2),
           answer_text    VARCHAR2(300),
           correct        VARCHAR2(2));
```

Next, you define VARRAY type vry_Answers, which stores Answer objects:

```
CREATE TYPE vry_Answers AS VARRAY(5) OF Answers;
```

Finally, you create relational table test_questions, which has a column of type vry_Answers, as follows:

```
CREATE TABLE test_questions (
           qst_id         NUMBER,
           test_id        VARCHAR2(10),
           question_text  VARCHAR2(100),
           answer_type    VARCHAR2(2),
           answers        vry_Answers);
```

Each item in column answers is a VARRAY that will store the answers to a given question. The relational table is populated in the following block. The VARRAY constructor vry_Answers() provides values for the answers column:

```
BEGIN
   INSERT INTO test_questions
      VALUES(1, '1Z0-051',
      'How many rows are returned by the SQL in the
exhibit?', 'S',
      vry_Answers(answers('A', '2 rows are returned', 'N'),
                  answers('B', '3 rows are returned', 'N'),
                  answers('C', '4 rows are returned', 'N'),
                  answers('D', 'No rows are returned', 'Y')
                  )
            );

   INSERT INTO test_questions
      VALUES(2, '1Z0-051',
      'A DELETE statement is an example of?', 'S',
      vry_Answers(answers('A', 'A DML statement', 'Y'),
                  answers('B', 'A DDL statement', 'N'),
                  answers('C', 'A DCL statement', 'N'),
                  answers('D', 'A TCL statement', 'N')
                  )
            );

   INSERT INTO test_questions
      VALUES(3, '1Z0-051', 'To format the SYSDATE to appear
         like ''05, February , 2013'', you would use?', 'S',
      vry_Answers(answers('A', 'TO_DATE(SYSDATE,
                                 ''DD, Month, YYYY'')', 'y'),
                  answers('B', 'TO_CHAR(SYSDATE,
                                 ''DD, Month, YYYY'')', 'N'),
                  answers('C', 'TRANSLATE(SYSDATE,
                                 ''DD, Month, YYYY'')', 'N'),
                  answers('D', 'DATEFUNC(SYSDATE,
                                 ''DD, Month, YYYY'')', 'N')
                     )
               );

END;
```

Question 3 has the wrong answer selected as correct. The following block creates a VARRY variable with the correct information and uses it to correct the data in the relational table.

```
DECLARE
   v_fix  vry_Answers :=
      vry_Answers(answers('A', 'TO_DATE(SYSDATE,
                          ''DD, Month, YYYY'')', 'N'),
                  answers('B', 'TO_CHAR(SYSDATE,
                          ''DD, Month, YYYY'')', 'Y'),
                  answers('C', 'TRANSLATE(SYSDATE,
                          ''DD, Month, YYYY'')', 'N'),
                  answers('D', 'DATEFUNC(SYSDATE,
                          ''DD, Month, YYYY'')', 'N'));
BEGIN
   UPDATE test_questions
   SET    answers = v_fix
   WHERE  qst_id = 3;
END;
```

Manipulating Individual Collection Elements

Both of the above examples manipulated the data in an entire collection. It is possible to use SQL to manipulate individual elements of a collection with the operator TABLE. The operand of TABLE is a subquery that returns a single column value for you to manipulate. TABLE can be used with either a nested table or a VARRAY. The following block adds another test to the oracle_certifications table for the SQL and PL/SQL test area:

```
BEGIN
   INSERT INTO
      TABLE(SELECT exams
            FROM   oracle_certifications
            WHERE  testing_area = 'SQL and PL/SQL')
      VALUES('1Z0-007', 'Introduction to Oracle9i SQL', 52,
120);
END;
```

An alternate way to have fixed the error with the swapped MySQL certification test IDs in the earlier nested table example for the oracle_certifications table is below. Instead of replacing the entire collection, the TABLE operator is used to locate and change the specific elements that are incorrect:

```
BEGIN
   UPDATE TABLE(SELECT exams
                FROM   oracle_certifications
                WHERE  testing_area = 'MySQL Developer')
   SET    test_id = '1Z0-871'
   WHERE  test_name LIKE 'MySQL%Part I';

   UPDATE TABLE(SELECT exams
                FROM   oracle_certifications
                WHERE  testing_area = 'MySQL Developer')
   SET    test_id = '1Z0-872'
   WHERE  test_name LIKE 'MySQL%Part II';
END;
```

However, it is not possible currently to reference the individual elements of a VARRAY in an INSERT, UPDATE, or DELETE statement. The problem with question three in the earlier VARRAY example could not have been resolved in this fashion. Accessing the individual elements of a VARRAY requires PL/SQL. The following block creates a local VARRAY variable and populates it with data from the incorrect relational table row. It then loops through the elements of the local VARRAY and corrects the data. Finally, it updates the row in the relational table with the local VARRAY variable:

```
DECLARE
    v_varray     vry_Answers;
BEGIN
   SELECT answers
   INTO   v_varray
   FROM   test_questions
   WHERE  qst_id = 3;

   FOR v_Lp IN v_varray.FIRST..v_varray.LAST LOOP
      IF v_varray(v_Lp).answer_id = 'A' THEN
         v_varray(v_Lp).correct := 'N';
      ELSIF v_varray(v_Lp).answer_id = 'B' THEN
         v_varray(v_Lp).correct := 'Y';
      END IF;
   END LOOP;

   UPDATE test_questions
   SET    answers = v_varray
   WHERE  qst_id = 3;
 END;
```

Distinguish between the different types of collections and their uses

One of the reasons for choosing one Oracle collection type over another is if you have legacy code or business logic in another language. One of the three PL/SQL collection types will usually directly translate from the other languages array and set types.

- **VARRAYs** -- Arrays in other languages will become VARRAYs.
- **Nested Tables** -- Sets and bags in other languages will translate best to Nested Tables.
- **Associative Arrays** -- Provide the best translation for hash tables and other kinds of unordered lookup tables in other languages.

If there is no legacy code to influence the decision, then the strengths and weaknesses of the three collections are the only means for choosing one over the others. When deciding between the collection types, it makes sense to perform the comparison between the types with the most common characteristics. Associative arrays and nested tables have several common factors, as do nested tables and VARRAYs.

It is possible to update individual elements of either associative arrays or nested tables. However, they have the following differences:

- Nested tables can be stored in a database column, but associative arrays cannot. If the data needs to be (or makes sense to be) stored in a relational table, then an associative array isn't the answer.
- Associative arrays work well for relatively small lookup tables if it is feasible (or desirable) for the collection to be constructed in memory when a procedure is called or a package is initialized.
- Associative arrays are good for collecting information whose volume is unknown beforehand.
- The index values of associative arrays are more flexible. The values can be negative, non-sequential, or be string values.
- PL/SQL automatically converts between host arrays and associative arrays that use numeric key values.

- Collections can be efficiently passed to and from the database server using associative arrays with bulk constructs (the FORALL statement or BULK COLLECT clause).

If the choice of a collection is between a nested table and a VARRAY, then the following factors should be considered:

VARRAYs are a good choice when:

- The number of elements is known in advance.
- The elements are usually all accessed in sequence.
- The ordering and subscripts must stay the same.

All elements of a VARRAY must be updated or retrieved at the same time. This is most desirable when performing some operation on all the elements at once. However, the larger the number of elements stored in a VARRAY, the less practical this restriction becomes.

Nested tables are a good choice when:

- The index values are not consecutive.
- There is no set number of index values, but a maximum limit is imposed.
- You need to delete or update some elements, but not all the elements at once.
- The alternative is to create a separate lookup table, with multiple entries for each row of the main table, to be accessed through join queries.
- Nested tables can be sparse: you can delete arbitrary elements, rather than just removing an item from the end.

Nested table data is held in a separate store table generated by the system and associated with the main table. The order and subscripts of a nested table cannot be guaranteed to remain stable as the nested table is stored in and retrieved from the database.

Using Advanced Interface Methods

Execute external C programs from PL/SQL

An external procedure is a procedure stored in a dynamic link library (DLL), or libunit for a Java class method. PL/SQL subprograms have the capability to an external procedure. When executed, the 3GL will be run in a separate address space from that of the database. The PL/SQL language is specialized for SQL transaction processing. Many computation-intensive tasks run more efficiently when executed in a lower-level language such as C.

Using PL/SQL external procedures, it is possible to write C procedure calls as PL/SQL bodies which can then be called directly from PL/SQL through the call specification interface. This service is designed for intercommunication between SQL, PL/SQL, C, and Java. The external procedure is registered with the base language, and then called when required to perform special-purpose processing. When called by PL/SQL, the language loads the library dynamically, and then calls the external procedure as if it were a PL/SQL subprogram. External procedures provide the following advantages:

- Isolate execution of client applications and processes from the database instance.
- Move computation-intensive tasks from client to server where they run faster.
- Interface the database server with external systems and data sources.
- Extend the functionality of the database server itself.
- They can be use to provide standard functionality for multiple databases.

Before external C procedures are available to PL/SQL they must be loaded. When an external C procedure is called, the Oracle Database or Oracle Listener starts the external procedure agent, extproc. The application will use the network connection established by Oracle to pass the following information to extproc:

- Name of DLL or shared library
- Name of external procedure
- Any parameters for the external procedure

After the above information has been received, extproc will load the DLL and run the external procedure. Any values returned by the external procedure will be passed back to the application. The call to the external procedure from PL/SQL is referred to as a callout. If the external procedure calls back to the database to perform SQL operations, this is known as a callback. The application and extproc must reside on the same computer. In order to use external procedures that are written in C, or that can be called from C applications, the following steps are required:

1. **Define the C Procedures** -- The C procedures must be defined using one of the following prototypes:
   - ✓ Kernighan & Ritchie style
   - ✓ ISO/ANSI prototypes other than numeric data types that are less than full width
   - ✓ Other data types that do not change size under default argument promotions.
2. **Set Up the Environment** -- The steps to configure the configuration files tnsnames.ora and listener.ora to use external procedures that are written in C, or can be called from C applications is beyond the scope of this guide (and almost certainly of the exam as well). You can find the details in the Advanced Application Developer's Guide.
3. **Identify the DLL** -- There are a number of security concerns with executing external programs security reasons. The DBA controls access to the DLL through the use of an alias library created with the CREATE LIBRARY statement. The alias library represents the DLL and allows the DBA to control EXECUTE access to the external procedure.
4. **Publish the External Procedures** -- External procedures are published through a call specification. The call specification maps names, parameter types, and return types for the C external

procedure to their SQL counterparts. The block for an external procedure is similar to a standard PL/SQL stored procedure except that, in its body, instead of declarations and a BEGIN END block, it uses the AS LANGUAGE clause.

The following steps show the basic process to execute an external stored procedure. The C code is just a placeholder for the example. I have not tried to compile it, and the exam is not going to get down to the level of debugging C procedures, so it is irrelevant.

1. Add a callout listener to your tnsnames.ora file:

```
(PROGRAM = extproc)
   (ENV =
"EXTPROC_DLLS=ONLY:/<filepath>/writefile1.so,LD_LIBRARY_PA
TH=/lib")
```

2. Create a shared library.

```
#include <stdio.h>
void writefile(char *p_path, char *p_text) {
   FILE *v_filename;
   v_filename = fopen(p_path,"w");
   fprintf(v_filename,"%s\n",p_text);
   fclose(v_filename); }
```

3. Compile the shared library:

```
gcc -shared -o writefile1.so writefile1.c
```

4. Create an alias library to point to the shared library file.

```
CREATE OR REPLACE LIBRARY lib_writefile
AS '/<filepath>/writefile1.so
```

5. Create a wrapper for the library.

```
CREATE OR REPLACE PROCEDURE c_writefile (p_path   VARCHAR2,
```

```
                                         p_text    VARCHAR2
  )
  AS EXTERNAL LIBRARY lib_writefile
  NAME "writefile"
  PARAMETERS
  (p_path STRING, p_text STRING);
```

5. Call the wrapper procedure from a PL/SQL block:

```
BEGIN
  c_writefile('/tmp/test.txt','Must pass test!');
END;
/
```

Execute Java programs from PL/SQL

Unlike the DLLs for C libraries, Java binaries and resources are actually stored in the database rather than being executed externally. The loadjava utility is used to load these into a system-generated database table. The command to do this would be:

```
> loadjava -user ocp/ocp Empfunc.class
```

The loadjava utility implicitly executes the SQL command CREATE JAVA. Alternately, you could explicitly use that command to load the Java resources into the database if an Oracle DIRECTORY object exists for the location where the OS file exists (java_dir in the following example is the name of a DIRECTORY object):

```
CREATE JAVA CLASS USING BFILE (java_dir, 'Empfunc.class');
```

Once the java resources are in the database, the steps for publishing a Java method are very similar to the steps for publishing a C procedure outlined in the previous section. You must define a stored PL/SQL subprogram with a call specification that maps the name, inputs and outputs of the external subprogram to PL/SQL equivalents. For this example, the Java class, Empfunc, is stored in the database:

```
import java.sql.*;
import oracle.jdbc.driver.*;
public class Empfunc {
  public static void setManager (int empNo, int mgrId)
```

```
    throws SQLException {
    Connection conn = new OracleDriver().defaultConnection();
    String sql = "UPDATE hr.employees
                  SET manager_id = ?
                  WHERE  employee_id = ?";
    try {
        PreparedStatement psql = conn.prepareStatement(sql);
        psql.setint(1, mgrId);
        psql.setInt(2, empNo);
        psql.executeUpdate();
        psql.close();
        } catch (SQLException e)
      {System.err.println(e.getMessage());}
    }
}
```

The class in this example has a single method, setManager. The method sets the manager ID value for a given employee. SetManager is a void method and returns no value when called and should be published as a PL/SQL procedure rather than as a function. To publish the method, a PL/SQL procedure must be created to map to the method:

```
CREATE OR REPLACE PROCEDURE emp_set_mgr (p_empid   NUMBER,
                                         p_mgrid   NUMBER)
AS
LANGUAGE JAVA
NAME 'Empfunc.setManager (int, int)';
/
```

The **emp_set_mgr** procedure can now be called from a PL/SQL block:

```
BEGIN
   -- Invoke Java method to set the manager ID of employee 128
   emp_set_mgr(128, 121);
END;
/
```

Implementing Fine-Grained Access Control for VPD

Explain the process of fine-grained access control

Oracle Virtual Private Database (VPD) allows for the creation of security policies to control access at the row and column levels. When configured, VPD will add WHERE conditions dynamically to SQL statements issued against tables, views, or synonyms that have had a security policy applied to them. The security policies are applied automatically on any access to the object, so bypassing the security is not possible. At the time of access -- whether direct or indirect -- to an object protected by an Oracle Virtual Private Database policy, a dynamic WHERE condition (called a predicate) is generated by a predefined function and added to the WHERE clause before the SQL is parsed. Oracle Virtual Private Database policies can be applied to SELECT, INSERT, UPDATE, INDEX, and DELETE statements.

If a VPD policy were to be created restricting access to records in the EMPLOYEES table to a given manager, a query issued by a user might be:

```
SELECT *
FROM   hr.employees;
```

A Virtual Private Database policy could be created to dynamically append a WHERE condition for the appropriate manager. For example:

```
SELECT *
FROM   hr.employees
WHERE  manager_id = 121;
```

Any query executed against the EMPLOYEES table would have this WHERE condition appended, so no records for managers other than 121 would ever be returned for this user.

Oracle's Virtual Private Database has several advantages over implementing data controls through an application interface:

- **Security** -- Because VPD policies are associated with a database table, view, or synonym, the access method is unimportant. When

access control is implemented at an application level, if users use a low-level tool such as SQL*Plus or SQL*Developer, they might be able to view or change data that they should not have access to.
- **Simplicity** -- A security policy is added to a table a single time. An application might require implementing an equivalent filter in numerous different locations to achieve the same effect.
- **Flexibility** -- It is possible to have different VPD policies for INSERT, DELETE, UPDATE, and SELECT statements. Different policies can be in effect based on user roles or even user-independent factors such as time of day or day of the week.

Policy functions can affect database performance if repeatedly executed. It is possible to reduce the impact of implementing policy functions by configuring how Oracle Virtual Private Database predicates are cached. There are three options available:

- Evaluate the policy once for each query (static policies).
- Evaluate the policy only when an application context within the policy function changes (context-sensitive policies).
- Evaluate the policy each time it is run (dynamic policies).

The dynamic WHERE clause (predicate) of a VPD policy is generated through a PL/SQL function (a procedure cannot be used). The return value of the function contains the restrictions that are to be applied. The function is normally created in the schema of the administrator in charge of security. The function created must meet the following requirements:

- It must take a schema name and an object (table, view, or synonym) name as inputs. The actual schema and object names should not be placed within the function. A policy created from the DBMS_RLS package will provide the function with the names of the schema, and object for which the policy will apply. The parameter for the schema must be created first, followed by the parameter for the object.

- It must provide a return value for the WHERE clause predicate. The return value generated for the WHERE clause must be a VARCHAR2 data type. The value returned must be a valid WHERE clause.
- It must not select from a table within the associated policy function (i.e. if the policy is on the employees table, the associated function cannot perform a SELECT against employees).

Once a function has been created that generates the desired predicate, it needs to be associated with the table to which the WHERE clause is to be applied. This is done by configuring an Oracle Virtual Private Database policy. VPD policies are responsible for managing the Virtual Private Database function. Policies can be configured to specify the types of SQL statements or particular table columns affected. When users attempt to access the associated object, the policy is put into effect. The DBMS_RLS package is used to manage an Oracle Virtual Private Database policy. The DBMS_RLS Procedures are:

- **ADD_POLICY** -- Adds a policy to a table, view, or synonym
- **ENABLE_POLICY** -- Enables (or disables) a policy you previously added to a table, view, or synonym
- **REFRESH_POLICY** -- Invalidates cursors associated with nonstatic policies
- **DROP_POLICY** -- To drop a policy from a table, view, or synonym
- **CREATE_POLICY_GROUP** -- Creates a policy group
- **DELETE_POLICY_GROUP** -- Drops a policy group
- **ADD_GROUPED_POLICY** -- Adds a policy to the specified policy group
- **ENABLE_GROUPED_POLICY** -- Enables a policy within a group
- **REFRESH_GROUPED_POLICY** -- Parses again the SQL statements associated with a refreshed policy
- **DISABLE_GROUPED_POLICY** -- Disables a policy within a group
- **DROP_GROUPED_POLICY** -- Drops a policy that is a member of the specified group
- **ADD_POLICY_CONTEXT** -- Adds the context for the active application
- **DROP_POLICY_CONTEXT** -- Drops the context for the application

Implement and test fine-grained access control

The following set of steps will create and implement a fine-grained access policy using a database session-based application context. Two users matching records in the EMPLOYEES table from the Oracle HR sample schema will be created. The VPD policy will ensure that any queries they make to the EMPLOYEES table will return only their direct reports.

Create the User Accounts

The example requires a database account to serve as the VPD administrator and the two manager accounts. The VPD administrator will require several privileges in order to create the required policies.

```
CREATE USER vpd_admin IDENTIFIED BY password;
GRANT   CREATE SESSION, CREATE ANY CONTEXT, CREATE PROCEDURE,
        CREATE TRIGGER, ADMINISTER DATABASE TRIGGER
TO      vpd_admin;

GRANT EXECUTE ON DBMS_SESSION TO vpd_admin;
GRANT EXECUTE ON DBMS_RLS TO vpd_admin;

CREATE USER ahunold IDENTIFIED BY password
GRANT CREATE SESSION TO ahunold;

CREATE USER ngreenbe IDENTIFIED BY password
GRANT CREATE SESSION TO ngreenbe;
```

All three users need SELECT privileges for hr.employees:

```
GRANT SELECT ON hr.employees TO vpd_admin;
GRANT SELECT ON hr.employees TO ahunold;
GRANT SELECT ON hr.employees TO ngreenbe;
```

At this point, both AHUNOLD and NGREENEBE can connect to the database and query all of the records in HR.EMPLOYEES:

```
SQL> CONNECT
Enter user-name: ahunold
Enter password:
Connected.
```

```
SQL> SELECT COUNT(*) FROM hr.employees;

  COUNT(*)
----------
       108

SQL> CONNECT
Enter user-name: ngreenbe
Enter password:
Connected.
SQL> SELECT COUNT(*) FROM hr.employees;

  COUNT(*)
----------
       108
```

Create a Database Session-Based Application Context

While connected as the VPD administrator, create an application context. While a context is associated with the schema that creates it, the owner of the context is always the SYS schema.

```
CREATE OR REPLACE CONTEXT emp_managers_ctx USING
employees_ctx;
```

Create a PL/SQL Package to Set the Application Context

Create a PL/SQL package while connected as the VPD administrator to set the database session-based application context. The package will be called when users login to the database. The set_empid procedure below queries the hr.employees table for records where the email matches that of the current database user name. If a record is found in the table, an application context value is set for the user with their employee ID.

```
CREATE OR REPLACE PACKAGE employees_ctx
IS
   PROCEDURE set_empid;
END;
/

CREATE OR REPLACE PACKAGE BODY employees_ctx
IS
PROCEDURE set_empid
AS
```

```
  v_emp_id     NUMBER;
BEGIN
  SELECT employee_id
  INTO   v_emp_id
  FROM   hr.employees
  WHERE  email = SYS_CONTEXT('USERENV', 'SESSION_USER');

  DBMS_SESSION.SET_CONTEXT('emp_managers_ctx', 'manager_id',
                           v_emp_id);
EXCEPTION
  WHEN NO_DATA_FOUND THEN
    NULL;
END set_empid;
END;
/
```

Create a Trigger to Run the Application Context Procedure

The context must be set every time a user logs into the database. This is effected by creating a logon trigger while connected to the VPD admin schema as follows:

```
CREATE TRIGGER tr_empid_ctx AFTER LOGON ON DATABASE
BEGIN
  vpd_admin.employees_ctx.set_empid;
END;
/
```

Create a PL/SQL Policy Function

The following function will return the predicate to filter the results from queries against the hr.employees table. It returns a WHERE predicate that translates to "where the employees displayed are managed by the current user." The WHERE predicate is appended to any queries run in the current session against the hr.employees table. The function is created in the VPD admin schema.

```
CREATE OR REPLACE FUNCTION filter_by_mgr(p_schema   IN
VARCHAR2,
                                         p_table    IN
VARCHAR2)
RETURN VARCHAR2
AS
  v_emp_pred    VARCHAR2 (400);
BEGIN
  v_emp_pred := 'manager_id = SYS_CONTEXT(''employees_ctx'',
''manager_id'')';
  RETURN v_emp_pred;
END;
/
```

Create the Security Policy

As user sysadmin_vpd, create the policy using the DBMS_RLS.ADD_POLICY procedure. The block below creates a policy named mgr_emp_filt and applies it to the hr.employees table. The policy is implemented by the filter_by_mgr function, which is stored in the vpd_admin schema. In addition to applying the predicate, the policy restricts users to issuing SELECT statements only against the table.

```
BEGIN
  DBMS_RLS.ADD_POLICY (object_schema    => 'hr',
                       object_name      => 'employees',
                       policy_name      => 'mgr_emp_filt',
                       function_schema  => 'vpd_admin',
                       policy_function  => 'filter_by_mgr',
                       statement_types  => 'select');
END;
/
```

Testing the Policy

Testing the policy is a matter of connecting as one of the two users and querying the hr.employees table. The check below first connects as user AHUNOLD and verifies that the context has been set. Then it gets a count of the rows visible in the employees table, and then queries the records.

```
SQL> CONNECT
Enter user-name: ahunold
Enter password:
Connected.


SELECT SYS_CONTEXT('emp_managers_ctx', 'manager_id') AS
MGR_ID
FROM dual;

MGR_ID
-------
103


SELECT COUNT(*)
FROM   hr.employees;

  COUNT(*)
----------
         4

SELECT employee_id, first_name, last_name, manager_id
FROM   hr.employees;

EMPLOYEE_ID FIRST_NAME     LAST_NAME      MANAGER_ID
----------- -------------- -------------- ----------
        104 Bruce          Ernst                 103
        105 David          Austin                103
        106 Valli          Pataballa             103
        107 Diana          Lorentz               103
```

Everything worked as expected for AHUNOLD. If one worked, the other is certain to. However, the same checks are run for user NGREENBE below:

```
SQL> connect ngreenbe
Enter password:
Connected.

SELECT SYS_CONTEXT('emp_managers_ctx', 'manager_id') AS
MGR_ID
FROM dual;

MGR_ID
-------
108
```

```
SELECT COUNT(*)
FROM   hr.employees;

  COUNT(*)
----------
         5

SELECT employee_id, first_name, last_name, manager_id
FROM   hr.employees;

EMPLOYEE_ID FIRST_NAME    LAST_NAME       MANAGER_ID
----------- ------------- --------------- ----------
        109 Daniel        Faviet                 108
        110 John          Chen                   108
        111 Ismael        Sciarra                108
        112 Jose Manuel   Urman                  108
        113 Luis          Popp                   108
```

Manipulating Large Objects

Create and manage LOB data types

All of the LOB data types with the exception of BFILES have the following characteristics:

- They store a LOB locator, which points to the location of the LOB data.
- They participate fully in transactions, are recoverable, and can be replicated.
- Changes made by package DBMS_LOB can be committed or rolled back.
- LOB locators can span transactions (for reads only), but they cannot span sessions.

None of the LOB data types can exceed 4 Gigabytes in length. The four types of LOB data types are:

- **CLOB** -- The CLOB data type is used to store large blocks of character data in the database, in-line or out-of-line. It supports either fixed-width or variable-width character sets. It is interpreted by the database as a single-byte character stream.
- **NCLOB** -- The NCLOB data type is used to store large blocks of NCHAR data in the database, in-line or out-of-line. It supports either fixed-width or variable-width character sets. It is interpreted by the database as a multi-byte character stream.
- **BLOB** -- The BLOB data type is used to store large binary objects in the database, in-line or out-of-line. It is interpreted by the database as a bit stream.
- **BFILE** -- The BFILE data type is used to store large binary objects in operating system files outside the database. The BFILE variable stores a file locator that points to an operating system file on the server. The locator includes a directory alias, which specifies a full path name. BFILEs cannot be

modified by Oracle. BFILEs do not participate in transactions, are not recoverable, and cannot be replicated. The maximum number of open BFILEs is set by the Oracle initialization parameter SESSION_MAX_OPEN_FILES, which is system dependent.

Oracle performs implicit conversion between CLOB and VARCHAR2 values. It cannot perform implicit conversion between other data types involving LOBS (i.e. CLOB to BLOB, BFILE to BLOB, VARCHAR2 to BLOB, etc.) There is some support for management of LOBs via SQL. However, a number of functions require the use of PL/SQL. The DBMS_LOB package provides the capability to more fully interact with LOB data types.

Internal LOBs store data in the Oracle database itself in the datafiles of tablespaces. The internal LOB types are:

- **CLOB (character LOB)** -- Stores large amounts of text in the database character set.
- **NCLOB (national character set LOB)** -- Stores Unicode data.
- **BLOB (binary LOB)** -- Stores large amounts of binary information as a bit stream.

Internal LOBs are stored differently from other data types. When a LOB column is created, a LOB segment and a LOB index are simultaneously created. The LOB segment and LOB index are always stored in the same tablespace, but this may be a different tablespace from the one contains the rest of the table. Data in a LOB segment is stored in pieces called chunks. This is a logically contiguous set of data blocks and is the smallest unit of allocation for a LOB. The row of the table where the LOB is defined stores a pointer called a LOB locator. The locator in turn points to the LOB index. When the table is queried, the LOB index is used to locate the required LOB chunks.

The only external LOB is a BFILE. When a BFILE column is added to the table, the database uses the column to store a pointer to a file in the operating system. The Oracle database can read from the operating system file but not write to it. Directory objects are used in conjunction with BFILEs to locate data. The amount of space that a BFILE consumes in the database is dependent on the length of the directory object name and the length of the file name. Because the BFILE is external to the database, it cannot make use of the same read consistency mechanism as internal LOBS. If data in the external file changes, repeated reads from the same file may produce different results.

Oracle provides read-only byte stream access to data stored in BFILEs. They can be accessed from any storage device accessible by your operating system, including hard disk drives, CD-ROMs, and DVDs. The database can access the data if the operating system supports stream-mode access to the files. BFILEs are typically used to hold:

- Binary data that does not change while your application is running, such as graphics.
- Data that is stored externally before being loaded into internal LOBs, where the data can then be manipulated.
- Data that is appropriate for byte-stream access, such as multimedia.
- Read-only data that is relatively large in size, to avoid taking up large amounts of room in tablespaces.

When creating a directory object or BFILEs, the following conditions must be met:

- The OS file must not be a symbolic or hard link.
- The OS directory path used by the DIRECTORY object must exist.
- The OS directory path used by the DIRECTORY object should not contain any symbolic links.

- The BFILENAME() function must be passed the directory object and filename in order to create a LOB locator that points to the external file.

The initialization parameter, SESSION_MAX_OPEN_FILES defines the maximum number of simultaneously open files in a session. The number of BFILES open is counted in that total. The parameter defaults to ten. If the number of unclosed files reaches the SESSION_MAX_OPEN_FILES value, no more can be opened until one or more open files is closed. To close all open files in a session, use the DBMS_LOB.FILECLOSEALL call.

In order to make use of BFILES, you must create one or more Oracle Directory objects. Oracle directories are database objects that specify an alias for a directory on the server file system. Once created, directories can be used to reference external binary file LOBs (BFILEs) and external tables files in the operating system directory aliased by them. Directory objects share a single namespace and are not owned by an individual schema.

Update LOBs with SQL

Data in CLOB columns can be updated directly and easily from SQL statements. There is no need to make use of any conversions or the DBMS_LOB package for CLOB operations:

```
CREATE TABLE ocp_articles (
article_id          NUMBER,
article_text        CLOB);

INSERT INTO ocp_articles
VALUES (10, 'This is a really short article');
1 rows inserted.
```

```
SELECT * FROM ocp_articles;

ARTICLE_ID ARTICLE_TEXT
---------- -------------------------------
        10 This is a really short article
```

It is also possible to use the BFILENAME function in the VALUES clause of an INSERT or UPDATE operation to populate a row with a LOB locator for an external file.

```
CREATE TABLE ocp_load_target (
load_id         NUMBER,
load_file       BFILE);

INSERT INTO ocp_load_target
VALUES (10, BFILENAME('C_TEMP', 'small_image.jpg'));
1 rows inserted.


SELECT * FROM ocp_load_target;

LOAD_ID LOAD_FILE
------- ----------
     10 (BFILE)

UPDATE ocp_load_target
SET    load_file = BFILENAME('C_TEMP', 'large_image.jpg')
WHERE  load_id = 10;

1 rows updated.
```

When inserting or updating rows into a table that contains CLOB or BLOB columns, the functions EMPTY_CLOB() and EMPTY_BLOB() can be used to initialize the columns to empty.

```
UPDATE ocp_articles_b
SET    article_text = EMPTY_BLOB()
WHERE  article_id = 10;

1 rows updated.
```

Just as you can INSERT values directly into CLOB columns via SQL, the UPDATE statement can be used directly. Effectively Oracle is implicitly converting the text (VARCHAR) data in the SQL statement to the CLOB data type.

```
UPDATE ocp_articles
SET    article_text = 'A change to the CLOB data'
WHERE  article_id = 10;
```

The SUBSTR and TRIM functions of the DBMS_LOB package can be used to display a portion of a LOB:

```
SELECT article_id,
       DBMS_LOB.SUBSTR (article_text, 1, 10) AS TEXT_PART
FROM   ocp_articles;

ARTICLE_ID TEXT_PART
---------- ------------
        10 A change t
```

Data from a CLOB column can be selected into a VARCHAR variable in a PL/SQL block providing the variable is large enough to hold it. Oracle will implicitly convert the data type to VARCHAR2:

```
DECLARE
  v_retval    VARCHAR2(300);
BEGIN
  SELECT article_text
  INTO   v_retval
  FROM   ocp_articles
  WHERE  article_id = 10;

  DBMS_OUTPUT.PUT_LINE(v_retval);
END;

A change to the CLOB data
```

BLOB or BFILE data cannot be displayed as the result of a SELECT operation. The data cannot be implicitly converted to something that can be displayed by the environment. Depending on how the particular development tool processes the results, it may return an error if you include a BLOB or BFILE column in a SELECT or it may display some innocuous result (I.e. '(BFILE)', or '(BLOB)').

To remove the LOB locator for a row and set the content of the column to empty, use the EMPTY_CLOB() or EMPTY_BLOB() functions:

```
UPDATE ocp_articles
SET    article_text = EMPTY_CLOB()
WHERE  article_id = 10;

1 rows updated.


UPDATE ocp_articles_b
SET    article_text = EMPTY_BLOB()
WHERE  article_id = 10;

1 rows updated.
```

Rows containing LOBs can be deleted exactly as you would rows that do not contain LOBs.

```
DELETE FROM ocp_articles_b
WHERE  article_id = 10;
1 rows deleted.
```

Use the DBMS_LOB PL/SQL package

The Oracle-supplied DBMS_LOB package provides a large number of subprograms that allow you to manipulate LOB data types, including BLOBs, CLOBs, NCLOBs, BFILEs, and temporary LOBs. DBMS_LOB can be used to access or manipulate specific parts of a LOB or complete LOBs. It can read and modify BLOBs, CLOBs, and NCLOBs, and provides read-only access to BFILEs. All of the subprograms in DBMS_LOB work through LOB locators. For any of the LOB operations to succeed, a valid LOB locator must be passed to them. To work with anything other than temporary LOBs, you must create tables with LOB columns, either internal or external, before DBMS_LOB will be able to work with them. The DBMS_LOB package does not perform any concurrency control on rows being updated. When updating rows, you should use the SELECT FOR UPDATE or a similar mechanism to lock any rows that contain LOBs that will be updated by DBMS_LOB in order to provide for concurrency.

The DBMS_LOB package contains a number of subprograms, including the following:

- **APPEND** -- This procedure appends the contents of the source LOB to the destination LOB.
- **CLOSE** -- This Procedure closes a previously opened internal or external LOB.
- **COMPARE** -- This function compares two entire LOBs or parts of two LOBs.
- **COPY** -- This procedure copies all, or part, of the source LOB to the destination LOB.
- **ERASE** -- This procedure erases all or part of a LOB.
- **FILECLOSE** -- This procedure closes the file.
- **FILECLOSEALL** -- This procedure closes all previously opened files.
- **FILEEXISTS** -- This function checks if the file exists on the server.
- **FILEGETNAME** -- This procedure gets the directory alias and file name.
- **FILEISOPEN** -- This function checks if the file was opened using the input BFILE locators.
- **FILEOPEN** -- This procedure opens a file.
- **GETLENGTH** – This function returns the length of the LOB.
- **INSTR** – This function returns the matching position of the nth occurrence of a pattern in the LOB.
- **SUBSTR** – This function returns a portion of the specified LOB.

- **ISOPEN** -- This function checks to see if the LOB was already opened using the input locator.
- **ISTEMPORARY** -- This function checks if the locator is pointing to a temporary LOB.
- **LOADFROMFILE** -- This procedure loads BFILE data into an internal LOB.
- **LOADBLOBFROMFILE** -- This procedure loads BFILE data into an internal BLOB.
- **LOADCLOBFROMFILE** -- This procedure loads BFILE data into an internal CLOB.
- **OPEN** -- This procedure opens a LOB (internal, external, or temporary) in the indicated mode.
- **READ** -- This procedure on reads data from the LOB starting at the specified offset.
- **WRITE** -- This procedure writes data to the LOB from a specified offset.
- **WRITEAPPEND** -- This procedure writes a buffer to the end of a LOB.

The subprograms in the DBMS_LOB package can be broken out into two types. The first type reads LOB data (COMPARE, FILEEXISTS, FILEGETNAME, FILEISOPEN, GETLENGTH, INSTR, READ, SUBSTR) and known as observers. The second type can alter LOB values (APPEND, COPY, ERASE, FILECLOSE, FILECLOSEALL, FILEOPEN, TRIM, WRITE) and are known as mutators.

The function below uses several subprograms from the DBMS_LOB package to create a REPLACE function that works for CLOB values similar to the functionality provided by the SQL REPLACE function:

```
CREATE FUNCTION clob_replace(p_clob      CLOB,
                             p_fromval   VARCHAR2,
                             p_toval     VARCHAR2 )
RETURN CLOB IS
  c_fromLen      CONSTANT PLS_INTEGER := LENGTH(p_fromval);
  c_toLen        CONSTANT PLS_INTEGER := LENGTH(p_toval);

  v_return       CLOB;
  v_segment      CLOB;
  v_position     PLS_INTEGER := 1 - c_toLen;
  v_offset       PLS_INTEGER := 1;
BEGIN
  IF p_fromval IS NOT NULL THEN
    WHILE v_offset < DBMS_LOB.GETLENGTH(p_clob) LOOP
      v_segment := DBMS_LOB.SUBSTR(p_clob, 32767, v_offset);
      LOOP
        v_position := DBMS_LOB.INSTR(v_segment, p_fromval,
                                     v_position + c_toLen);
        EXIT WHEN (NVL(v_position,0) = 0)
              OR (v_position = 32767-c_toLen);
        v_segment := TO_CLOB( DBMS_LOB.SUBSTR(v_segment,
                                              v_position-1)
                              || p_toval
                              || DBMS_LOB.SUBSTR(v_segment,
                                 32767 - c_fromLen - v_position -
                                 c_fromLen+1,v_position+c_fromLen));
      END LOOP;

      v_return := v_return || v_segment;
      v_offset := v_offset + 32767 - c_fromLen;
    END LOOP;
  END IF;

  RETURN(v_return);
END;
```

You can use the UTL_FILE package to read a binary file into a PL/SQL BLOB variable and then insert that value into a BLOB column. Alternately, you can use a BFILE to point to the external file and then use the DBMS_LOB procedure LOADBLOBFROMFILE to pull the binary data in to Oracle. Since the second option is more in keeping with this topic, the example below does just that. The first section below creates a table to hold a row with a BFILE LOB locator pointing to the external file to be loaded and inserts a row pointing to an external JPG file:

```
CREATE TABLE ocp_load_target (
load_id           NUMBER,
load_file         BFILE);

INSERT INTO ocp_load_target
VALUES (10, BFILENAME('C_TEMP', 'small_image.jpg'));
1 rows inserted.


SELECT * FROM ocp_load_target;

LOAD_ID LOAD_FILE
------- ----------
     10 (BFILE)
```

While you can create a BLOB column via SQL, populating it directly with a text string generates an error. You could use the RAWTOHEX function to convert the string to hexadecimal and bypass the error but it would be pointless. BLOB columns are for storing binary data, not character data.

```
CREATE TABLE ocp_articles_b (
article_id            NUMBER,
article_text          BLOB);

INSERT INTO ocp_articles_b
VALUES (10, 'This is a really short article');

Error report:
SQL Error: ORA-01465: invalid hex number
01465. 00000 -  "invalid hex number"
*Cause:
*Action:
```

Populating a bloc column in a table requires a source of binary data. The procedure below uses the DBMS_LOB package to read the binary data from the external file into a BLOB variable. The binary data in the variable is then inserted into the BLOB column of the table created in the earlier example:

```
CREATE PROCEDURE load_ocp_articles_b (p_article_id  NUMBER)
AS
  v_bfile         BFILE :=
BFILENAME('C_TEMP','small_image.jpg');
  v_Title         VARCHAR2(100);
  v_OffSetIn      INTEGER := 1;
  v_OffSetFrom    INTEGER := 1;
  v_blob          BLOB;
BEGIN
  SELECT load_file
  INTO   v_bfile
  FROM   ocp_load_target
  WHERE  load_id = 10;

  DBMS_LOB.CREATETEMPORARY (v_blob, true);
  DBMS_LOB.OPEN(v_bfile, DBMS_LOB.LOB_READONLY);
  DBMS_LOB.OPEN(v_blob, DBMS_LOB.LOB_READWRITE);
  DBMS_LOB.LOADFROMFILE(v_blob, v_bfile, DBMS_LOB.LOBMAXSIZE,
                   v_OffSetIn, v_OffSetFrom);

  INSERT INTO ocp_articles_b
  VALUES (p_article_id, v_blob);

  DBMS_LOB.CLOSE(v_blob);
  DBMS_LOB.CLOSE(v_bfile);
END load_ocp_articles_b;


BEGIN
  load_ocp_articles_b(10);
END;

SELECT * FROM ocp_articles_b;

ARTICLE_ID ARTICLE_TEXT
---------- --------------
        10 (BLOB)
```

Use of temporary LOBs

A temporary LOB is a BLOB, CLOB, or NCLOB that persists only within the application scope in which it is declared. Temporary LOBs are not part of any database table. Oracle tracks the usage of temporary LOBs in each session. Information about temporary LOBs can be found in the view

V$TEMPORARY_LOBS. It is possible to use this view to determine the owner of the temporary LOB by identifying the session. The data for temporary LOBs is stored in a temporary tablespace. The space used will be freed at the end of the session that created the LOBs if they are not explicitly free before then. There are three subprograms in the DBMS_LOB package related to temporary LOBs:

- **CREATETEMPORARY** -- Creates a temporary LOB
- **ISTEMPORARY** -- Checks if a LOB locator refers to a temporary LOB
- **FREETEMPORARY** -- Frees a temporary LOB

In order to create a temporary LOB, a variable of the desired LOB data type must be declared. This variable is then passed to the CREATETEMPORARY procedure. The temporary LOB will then exist until one of three events occurs:

- The variable goes out of scope
- The session terminates.
- The temporary LOB is explicitly freed.

Freeing a temporary LOB instance explicitly is recommended to minimize system resource usage. The following block makes use of the DBMS_LOB package to create, identify, and free temporary LOBs via PL/SQL:

```
DECLARE
  v_clob      CLOB;
  v_blob      BLOB;
  v_nclob     NCLOB;
  v_clob2     CLOB;

  v_istemp    PLS_INTEGER;
BEGIN
  -- create temp LOBs
  DBMS_LOB.CREATETEMPORARY(v_clob, TRUE, DBMS_LOB.SESSION);
  DBMS_LOB.CREATETEMPORARY(v_blob, TRUE, DBMS_LOB.SESSION);
  DBMS_LOB.CREATETEMPORARY(v_nclob, TRUE, DBMS_LOB.SESSION);

  -- See if variable is temporary
  v_istemp := DBMS_LOB.ISTEMPORARY(v_clob);
```

```
  CASE v_istemp
    WHEN 1 THEN
      DBMS_OUTPUT.PUT_LINE('LOB v_clob is temporary.');
    WHEN 2 THEN
      DBMS_OUTPUT.PUT_LINE('LOB v_clob is *not* temporary.');
    ELSE
      DBMS_OUTPUT.PUT_LINE('LOB v_clob locator is NULL.');
  END CASE;

  -- See if variable is temporary
  v_istemp := DBMS_LOB.ISTEMPORARY(v_clob2);

  CASE v_istemp
    WHEN 1 THEN
      DBMS_OUTPUT.PUT_LINE('LOB v_clob2 is temporary.');
    WHEN 2 THEN
      DBMS_OUTPUT.PUT_LINE('LOB v_clob2 is *not*
temporary.');
    ELSE
      DBMS_OUTPUT.PUT_LINE('LOB v_clob2 locator is NULL.');
  END CASE;

  -- Free the temporary LOBs
  DBMS_LOB.FREETEMPORARY(v_clob);
  DBMS_LOB.FREETEMPORARY(v_blob);
  DBMS_LOB.FREETEMPORARY(v_nclob);
END;
/

Output:
LOB v_clob is temporary.
LOB v_clob2 locator is NULL.
```

The database administrator should set up a separate temporary tablespace for temporary LOB storage instead of the default system tablespace. Having a separate tablespace will minimize device contention when copying data from persistent LOBs to temporary LOBs. There are a number of cases where temporary LOBs are created implicitly in SQL and PL/SQL. The temporary tablespace for storing temporary LOBs must be large enough to provide sufficient storage.

Temporary LOBs are silently created when you use the following:

- SQL functions on LOBs
- PL/SQL built-in character functions on LOBs
- Variable assignments from VARCHAR2/RAW to CLOBs/BLOBs, respectively.
- Perform a LONG-to-LOB migration

Administering SecureFile LOBs

Describe SecureFile LOB features

In Oracle 11G Release 1, a new type of Large-Object storage was added, SecureFile LOBs. The legacy LOB format has been renamed to BasicFile LOBs. SecureFiles LOBs are created when the storage keyword SECUREFILE appears in the CREATE TABLE statement. BasicFile LOBs continue to be the default storage and will be in effect if the CREATE TABLE statement does not have the keyword SECUREFILE, or if the keyword BASICFILE is used. Writing to and reading from SecureFile LOBs is identical to BasicFile LOBs. SecureFile LOBs add several new capabilities to LOB data storage:

- **Compression** -- Intelligent LOB compression enables users to explicitly compress data to save disk space. You must have a license for the Oracle Advanced Compression Option before implementing SecureFiles Intelligent Compression.
- **Encryption** -- Intelligent LOB encryption allows encrypted data to be stored in-place and is available for random reads and writes. You must have a license for the Oracle Advanced Security Option before implementing SecureFiles Intelligent Encryption.
- **Deduplication** -- The deduplication option allows Oracle to automatically detect duplicate LOB data and conserve space by only storing a single copy of the data. You must have a license for the Oracle Advanced Compression Option before implementing SecureFiles Intelligent Deduplication.
- **Optimization** -- LOB data path optimization includes logical cache above storage layer, read prefetching, new caching modes, vectored IO, and more.

db_securefile parameter

The new init.ora parameter, db_securefile, is used to determine the behavior of the Oracle database in reference to using or not using SecureFile LOBs or BasicFile LOBs. The possible values of this parameter are: ALWAYS, FORCE, PERMITTED, NEVER, and IGNORE. The meaning of each of the values is:

- **ALWAYS** -- attempt to create SecureFile LOBs but fall back to BasicFile LOBs if the tablespace is not using ASSM.
- **FORCE** -- force all LOBs created going forward to be SecureFile LOBs. If the LOB is being created in an ASSM tablespace, an error will be thrown.
- **PERMITTED** -- allow SecureFile LOBs to be created
- **NEVER** -- disallow SecureFile LOBs from being created. If a DML statement tries to create a column as a SecureFile LOB, it will instead be created as a BasicFile LOB. If any SecureFile specific storage options or features are in the DML, an exception is created.
- **IGNORE** -- disallow SecureFile LOBs and ignore any errors that would otherwise be caused by forcing BasicFile LOBs with SecureFile options.

DBMS_LOB

SecureFiles inherit the LOB column settings for deduplication, encryption, and compression that were specified at the time the LOB was created. You can use the new procedures added to the DBMS_LOB package to determine or override the inherited values.

- **DBMS_LOB.GETOPTIONS** -- The current settings of a SecureFile LOB can be obtained using this function. An integer corresponding to a pre-defined constant based on the option type is returned. As an example, the value for DEDUPLICATE_OFF is 0. You won't need to know the values for the test. You might need to know the procedure name.
- **DBMS_LOB.SETOPTIONS** -- This procedure sets features of a SecureFile LOB (compression, deduplication, and encryption). It enables the features to be set on a per-LOB basis, overriding the default LOB settings.
- **DBMS_LOB.ISSECUREFILE** -- This function returns TRUE or FALSE depending on whether the LOB locator (BLOB or CLOB) passed to it is for a SecureFile.

DBMS_SPACE.SPACE_USAGE

The existing SPACE_USAGE procedure is overloaded to return information about LOB space usage. It returns the amount of disk space in blocks used by all the LOBs in the LOB segment. This procedure can only be used on tablespaces that are created with auto segment space management.

Enable SecureFile LOB deduplication, compression, and encryption

A SecureFiles LOB can only be created in a tablespace managed with Automatic Segment Space Management (ASSM). It is recommended that any desired compression, deduplication, or encryption be enabled in the CREATE TABLE statement. When these features are enabled through an ALTER TABLE statement, all SecureFiles LOB data in the table will be read, modified, and written. This operation will force the database to lock the table for an operation that may take a considerable amount of time. There are a number of parameters of the CREATE TABLE statement related to SecureFile LOBs:

- **BASICFILE** -- Specifies the original architecture for LOBs. It creates BasicFile LOBs, which do not support compression, deduplication or encryption features.
- **SECUREFILE** -- Specifies the use of the SecureFiles LOB storage architecture and functionality. A SecureFiles LOB can only be created in a tablespace managed with Automatic Segment Space Management (ASSM).
- **CHUNK** -- CHUNK is one or more Oracle blocks. For SecureFiles LOBs, CHUNK is an advisory size and is provided for backward compatibility purposes.
- **RETENTION** -- Specifies the retention policy.
    - ✓ **MAX** -- Oracle will keep old versions of LOB data blocks until the space used by the segment has reached the size specified in the MAXSIZE parameter. If MAXSIZE is not specified, MAX behaves like AUTO.
    - ✓ **MIN** -- Oracle will keep old versions of LOB data blocks for the specified number of seconds.

- ✓ **NONE** -- means that there is no retention period and space can be reused in any way deemed necessary.
- ✓ **AUTO** -- Oracle manages the space as efficiently as possible weighing both time and space needs.
- **MAXSIZE** -- Limits the amount of space that can be used by the LOB segment to the given size. If this size is consumed, new LOB data blocks are taken from the pool of old versions of LOB data blocks regardless of time requirements and as needed.
- **FREEPOOLS** -- Specifies the number of FREELIST groups for BasicFiles LOBs, if the database is in automatic undo mode. Under 11g compatibility, this parameter is ignored when SecureFiles LOBs are created.
- **LOGGING, NOLOGGING, or FILESYSTEM_LIKE_LOGGING** -- Determines redo logging behavior.
    - ✓ **LOGGING** -- The creation of the LOB, and subsequent inserts into the LOB, are logged in the redo log file. LOGGING is the default.
    - ✓ **NOLOGGING** -- LOB creation and inserts are not logged. For SecureFiles LOBs, the NOLOGGING setting is converted internally to FILESYSTEM_LIKE_LOGGING.
    - ✓ **FILESYSTEM_LIKE_LOGGING** -- The system only logs the metadata. It ensures that data is completely recoverable after a server failure. This option is invalid for BasicFiles LOBs.
- **FREELISTS or FREELIST GROUPS** -- This parameter specifies the number of process freelists or freelist groups, respectively, allocated to the segment.
- **PCTVERSION** -- This parameter specifies the percentage of all used BasicFiles LOB data space that can be occupied by old versions of BasicFiles LOB data pages.
- **COMPRESS or NOCOMPRESS** -- The COMPRESS option turns on SecureFiles Intelligent Compression, and NOCOMPRESS turns it off.
- **DEDUPLICATE or KEEP_DUPLICATES** -- The DEDUPLICATE option enables SecureFiles Intelligent Deduplication; it specifies that SecureFiles LOB data that is identical in two or more rows in a LOB column, partition or subpartition must share the same data blocks.
- **ENCRYPT or DECRYPT** -- The ENCRYPT option turns on SecureFiles Intelligent Encryption, and encrypts all SecureFiles LOB data using

Oracle Transparent Data Encryption (TDE). The DECRYPT option turns off SecureFiles Intelligent Encryption.

Compression

SecureFiles Intelligent Compression is not related to Oracle table or index compression. Enabling one does not affect the other. When enabling SecureFiles Intelligent Compression, there are options for LOW, MEDIUM and HIGH degrees of compression. As the amount of compression is increased, the CPU overhead increases but the compression level becomes more effective. MEDIUM compression is the default. LOW compression uses a lightweight compression algorithm that has a very small CPU cost. SecureFiles LOBs compressed at LOW generally consume less CPU time than BasicFile LOBs and generally run faster due to reduced disk I/O.

Create a SecureFiles LOB column with LOW compression

```
CREATE TABLE lowcomp (col1 CLOB)
LOB(col1) STORE AS SECUREFILE(
  COMPRESS LOW
  CACHE
);
```

Create a SecureFiles LOB column with MEDIUM (default) compression

```
CREATE TABLE medcomp (col1 CLOB)
LOB(col1) STORE AS SECUREFILE(
  COMPRESS
  CACHE
);
```

Creating a SecureFiles LOB column with disabled compression

```
CREATE TABLE nocomp (col1 CLOB)
LOB(col1) STORE AS SECUREFILE(
  NOCOMPRESS
  CACHE
);
```

Change SecureFiles LOB compression via ALTER TABLE

```
ALTER TABLE medcomp MODIFY
  LOB(col1) (COMPRESS LOW);
```

Deduplication

Duplicate detection occurs only within a single LOB segment. LOB columns duplicate detection does not span partitions or subpartitions and is applicable only to SecureFiles LOBs. After a SecureFiles LOB has been created, the DBMS_LOB.SETOPTIONS procedure can be used to enable or disable deduplication for individual LOBs.

Create a SecureFiles LOB column with deduplication

```
CREATE TABLE dedup (col1 CLOB)
LOB(col1) STORE AS SECUREFILE(
  DEDUPLICATE
  CACHE
);
```

Create a SecureFiles LOB column with disabled deduplication

```
CREATE TABLE keepdup (col1 CLOB)
LOB(col1) STORE AS SECUREFILE(
  KEEP_DUPLICATES
  CACHE
);
```

Altering a SecureFiles LOB column to disable deduplication

```
ALTER TABLE dedup MODIFY
   LOB(col1) (KEEP_DUPLICATES);
```

Encryption

The following factors apply to SecureFile Transparent Data Encryption:

- The current Transparent Data Encryption (TDE) syntax is used for enabling encryption on SecureFile LOB data types.
- LOB data is encrypted at the block level.
- Valid encryption algorithms are: AES192 (default), 3DES168, AES128, and AES256.
- The column encryption key is derived from PASSWORD, if specified.
- SALT is the default for LOB encryption. NO SALT is not supported.
- All LOBs in the LOB column are encrypted.
- LOBs can be encrypted only on a per-column basis. All partitions within a LOB column are encrypted.
- TDE is not supported by the traditional import and export utilities or by transportable-tablespace-based export. Use the Data Pump import and export utilities with encrypted columns instead.

Before it is possible to use Transparent Data Encryption, the security administrator must create a wallet and set a master key. It is possible to use the default database wallet shared by other Oracle Database components. Alternately, a separate wallet can be created for TDE. Oracle strongly recommends using a separate wallet to store the master encryption key. If the ENCRYPTION_WALLET_LOCATION parameter is not present in the sqlnet.ora file, then the WALLET_LOCATION value is used. If WALLET_LOCATION is not specified in the sqlnet.ora file, then the default database wallet location is used. The default database wallet location is ORACLE_BASE/admin/DB_UNIQUE_NAME/wallet.

To use a wallet specifically for TDE, a wallet location must be specified in the sqlnet.ora file by using the ENCRYPTION_WALLET_LOCATION parameter. The master encryption key is stored in an external security module. The master key is used to protect the table keys and tablespace encryption keys. By default, it is a random key generated by TDE. It can also be an existing key pair from a PKI certificate designated for encryption.

To set the master encryption key, use the following command:

```
ALTER SYSTEM SET ENCRYPTION KEY ["certificate_ID"] IDENTIFIED
BY "password";
```

- **certificate_ID** -- This is an optional string containing the unique identifier of a certificate stored in the Oracle wallet. Use this parameter if you intend to use your PKI private key as your master encryption key.
- **password** -- This is the mandatory wallet password for the security module. It is case sensitive.

The database must load the master encryption key into memory before it can encrypt or decrypt columns/tablespaces. The following ALTER SYSTEM command explicitly opens the wallet:

```
ALTER SYSTEM SET ENCRYPTION WALLET OPEN IDENTIFIED BY
"password"
```

The "password" value is the one used when the encryption key was created. The password string must be enclosed in double quotation marks. Once the wallet has been opened, it remains open until the database instance is shut down, or it is closed explicitly. The following command will explicitly close the wallet:

```
ALTER SYSTEM SET ENCRYPTION WALLET CLOSE IDENTIFIED BY
"password"
```

Closing the wallet disables all encryption and decryption operations. Each time you restart a database instance, the wallet must be opened to re-enable encryption and decryption operations. The data dictionary view USER_ENCRYPTED_COLUMNS can be used to determine which columns are encrypted and their status.

Create a SecureFiles LOB column with a specific encryption algorithm

```
CREATE TABLE tab_3DES (col1 CLOB ENCRYPT USING '3DES168')
LOB(col1) STORE AS SECUREFILE(
  CACHE
  NOLOGGING
);
```

Create a SecureFiles LOB column with encryption and a password key

```
CREATE TABLE tab_enc_pw (col1 CLOB ENCRYPT IDENTIFIED BY
badpassword)
LOB(col1) STORE AS SECUREFILE(
  CACHE
);
```

Enable LOB encryption using AES256.

```
ALTER TABLE tab_nocrypt MODIFY
  ( col1 CLOB ENCRYPT USING 'AES256');
```

Alter a SecureFiles LOB column by re-keying the encryption

```
ALTER TABLE tab_3DES REKEY USING 'AES256';
```

Disable LOB encryption

```
ALTER TABLE tab_enc_pw MODIFY
  ( col1 CLOB DECRYPT);
```

Migrate BasicFile LOBs to the SecureFile LOB format

It is possible to migrate data from BasicFile LOBs to SecureFile LOBs using any of several methods:

- Create table as Select (CTAS)
- Insert table as Select (ITAS)
- Export/Import

- Column to Column copy
- Online redefinition

Most of the migration options require additional disk space equal to at least the space used by the CLOB column, and some the space used by the entire table. For partitioned tables, performing the migration on a partition-by-partition basis can reduce the overall disk space requirement. Of the available solutions, the only one recommended by Oracle is online redefinition. Online redefinition can be performed at the table or partition level. The advantages and disadvantages to online redefinition are:

Advantages

- The table or partition does not need to be taken offline
- The redefinition can be performed in parallel

Disadvantages

- Additional storage equal to the entire table or partition and all LOB segments must be available
- After redefinition, any global indexes must be rebuilt

Migrating BasicFile LOBs to SecureFile LOBs can generate significant redo which may have performance implications. However, redo is generated during the migration only if the table has been set to LOGGING. Redo changes for the column being converted from BasicFile LOBs to SecureFile LOBs are logged only if the storage characteristics of the SecureFiles LOB column indicate LOGGING. The NOLOGGING storage parameter should be set for the new SecureFiles column before beginning the migration. Once the migration is complete, you can turn LOGGING back to the original setting.

Online Redefinition

Online redefinition requires the creation of an interim table for data storage during the transfer process. This table is declared with columns to hold all of the existing columns as they exist in the original table, with the exception of the LOB column being converted. That column will be created using the SecureFiles format with the settings you want the original table to have after redefinition. There is no need to create constraints on the interim table to match the original. The constraints from the original table will be used.

Once the interim table has been created, the DBMS_REDEFINITION package is used to perform the operation. There are three procedures that will be used to perform the redefinition:

- **START_REDEF_TABLE** -- Initiates the redefinition process
- **COPY_TABLE_DEPENDENTS** -- Copies the dependent objects of the original table onto the interim table
- **FINISH_REDEF_TABLE** -- Completes the redefinition process.

Prior to calling START_REDEF_TABLE, you must have already created an empty interim table in the same schema as the table to be redefined. The interim table should have the desired attributes of the post-redefinition table. once the table exists, call this procedure to initiate the redefinition process.

```
START_REDEF_TABLE (uname         IN VARCHAR2,
                   orig_table    IN VARCHAR2,
                   int_table     IN VARCHAR2,
                   col_mapping   IN VARCHAR2 := NULL,
                   options_flag  IN BINARY_INTEGER := 1,
                   orderby_cols  IN VARCHAR2 := NULL,
                   part_name     IN VARCHAR2 := NULL);
```

- **uname** -- Schema name the tables are in
- **orig_table** -- Name of the table to be redefined
- **int_table** -- Name of the interim table
- **col_mapping** -- Mapping information from the columns in the original table to the columns in the interim table. If NULL, all the

columns in the original table are selected and have the same name after redefinition.
- **options_flag** -- Indicates the type of redefinition method to use:
    - ✓ **dbms_redefinition.cons_use_pk (1)** -- The redefinition is done using primary keys. This is the default.
    - ✓ **dbms_redefinition.cons_use_rowid (2)** -- The redefinition is done using rowids.
- **orderby_cols** -- This optional parameter accepts the list of columns (along with the optional keyword(s) ascending/descending) with which to order by the rows during the initial instantiation of the interim table.
- **part_name** -- Name of the partition being redefined. If redefining only a single partition of a table, specify the partition name in this parameter. NULL implies the entire table is being redefined.

The COPY_TABLE_DEPENDENTS procedure clones the dependent objects of the table being redefined onto the interim table and registers the dependent objects. It clones the dependent objects (like grants, triggers, constraints and privileges) from the table being redefined to the interim table (which represents the post-redefinition table). The value returned by the **num_errors** OUT parameter should be checked after executing this procedure to ensure that no errors occurred during the cloning of the objects.

```
COPY_TABLE_DEPENDENTS(uname             IN VARCHAR2,
                     orig_table         IN VARCHAR2,
                     int_table          IN VARCHAR2,
                     copy_indexes       IN PLS_INTEGER := 1,
                     copy_triggers      IN BOOLEAN := TRUE,
                     copy_constraints   IN BOOLEAN := TRUE,
                     copy_privileges    IN BOOLEAN := TRUE,
                     ignore_errors      IN BOOLEAN := FALSE,
                     num_errors         OUT PLS_INTEGER,
                     copy_statistics    IN BOOLEAN := FALSE,
                     copy_mvlog         IN BOOLEAN := FALSE);
```

- **uname** -- Schema name of the tables
- **orig_table** -- Name of the table being redefined
- **int_table** -- Name of the interim table
- **copy_indexes**-- Flag indicating whether to copy the indexes

- ✓ **0** -- do not copy any index
- ✓ **dbms_redefinition.cons_orig_params** -– copy the indexes using the physical parameters of the source indexes
- **copy_triggers** -- TRUE = clone triggers, FALSE = do nothing
- **copy_constraints** -- TRUE = clone constraints, FALSE = do nothing.
- **copy_privileges** -- TRUE = clone privileges, FALSE = do nothing
- **ignore_errors** -- TRUE = if an error occurs while cloning a particular dependent object, then skip that object and continue cloning other dependent objects. FALSE = that the cloning process should stop upon encountering an error.
- **num_errors** -- Number of errors that occurred while cloning dependent objects
- **copy_statistics** -- TRUE = copy statistics, FALSE = do nothing
- **copy_mvlog** -- TRUE = copy materialized view log, FALSE = do nothing

The FINISH_REDEF_TABLE procedure completes the redefinition process. Prior to executing this procedure, you can create new indexes, triggers, grants, and constraints as desired on the interim table. The referential constraints involving the interim table must be disabled. After this procedure is run, the original table is redefined with the attributes and data of the interim table. The original table is locked briefly while FINISH_REDEF_TABLE executes.

```
FINISH_REDEF_TABLE (uname       IN VARCHAR2,
                    orig_table  IN VARCHAR2,
                    int_table   IN VARCHAR2,
                    part_name   IN VARCHAR2 := NULL);
```

- **uname** -- Schema name of the tables

- **orig_table** -- Name of the table to be redefined

- **int_table** -- Name of the interim table

- **part_name** -- Name of the partition being redefined. If redefining only a single partition of a table, specify the partition name in this parameter. NULL implies the entire table is being redefined.

The following example walks through an online redefinition. It creates a small table with four columns from the HR.EMPLOYEES table. The PHONE_NUMBER column is created as a BasicFile LOB for this example.

```
CREATE TABLE employees_lob (
employee_id    NUMBER(6),
first_name     VARCHAR2(20),
last_name      VARCHAR2(25),
phone_number   CLOB)


ALTER TABLE employees_lob
ADD CONSTRAINT employees_lob_pk
PRIMARY KEY (employee_id);


INSERT INTO employees_lob
(SELECT employee_id, first_name, last_name, phone_number
 FROM   hr.employees
 WHERE  job_id = 'AD_VP');


CREATE TABLE employees_int (
employee_id    NUMBER(6),
first_name     VARCHAR2(20),
last_name      VARCHAR2(25),
phone_number   CLOB)
LOB(phone_number) STORE AS SECUREFILE
                  (NOCACHE FILESYSTEM_LIKE_LOGGING);


DECLARE
  v_col_mapping    VARCHAR2(250);
BEGIN
  -- map all the columns in the interim table to the original table
  v_col_mapping := 'employee_id employee_id, '||
                   'first_name first_name, '||
                   'last_name last_name, '||
                   'phone_number phone_number';

  DBMS_REDEFINITION.START_REDEF_TABLE(
                 uname       =>  'ocpguru',
                 orig_table  =>  'employees_lob',
                 int_table   =>  'employees_int',
                 col_mapping =>  v_col_mapping);
END;
/
```

```
DECLARE
  v_errors       PLS_INTEGER := 0;
BEGIN
  DBMS_REDEFINITION.COPY_TABLE_DEPENDENTS(
                   uname         => 'ocpguru',
                   orig_table    => 'employees_lob',
                   int_table     => 'employees_int',
                   num_errors    => v_errors);

  DBMS_OUTPUT.PUT_LINE('# Errors: ' || TO_CHAR(v_errors));
END;
/

BEGIN
  DBMS_REDEFINITION.FINISH_REDEF_TABLE(
                   uname         => 'ocpguru',
                   orig_table    => 'employees_lob',
                   int_table     => 'employees_int');
END;
/

-- Drop the interim table
DROP TABLE employees_int;
```

Performance and Tuning

Use native and interpreted compilation methods

The execution of PL/SQL subprograms is generally faster when compiled into native code rather than the default of interpreted code. The definitions of the two compilation types are:

- **Interpreted** -- The statements in a PL/SQL unit are compiled into an intermediate form called system code. The system code is stored in the catalog. The system code will then be interpreted at run time.
- **Native compilation** -- The statements in a PL/SQL unit are compiled into native code (processor-dependent system code) and stored in the SYSTEM tablespace. There is no need for the native code to be interpreted at run time, so it executes faster.

Any PL/SQL unit of any type, including PL/SQL supplied with the Oracle Database can be natively compiled. Natively compiled program units work in all server environments and require no special set-up or maintenance on most platforms. On some platforms, the DBA might want to do some optional configuration. If you determine that PL/SQL native compilation will improve PL/SQL performance, Oracle recommends compiling the entire database for native mode. This requires DBA privileges, but will speed up both your own code and calls to the PL/SQL packages that Oracle Database supplies.

Native compilation applies only to PL/SQL statements and has no affect on SQL performance. If the majority of execution time for a given PL/SQL subprogram is related to SQL operations, native compilation will have little positive impact. However, the natively compiled code will run at least as fast as the corresponding interpreted code. When a natively compiled PL/SQL unit is first executed, it is fetched from the SYSTEM tablespace into shared memory. All sessions invoking that program unit will share a single copy of the code in shared memory. If a program unit is not being used, it may age out of the shared memory to reduce memory load. Natively compiled subprograms and interpreted subprograms can invoke each other. The compilation parameter PLSQL_CODE_TYPE determines whether PL/SQL code is natively compiled or interpreted.

Interpreted mode has two advantages over native compilation:

- PL/SQL debugging tools can be used on program units compiled for interpreted mode, but not unit compiled for native mode.
- Compiling for interpreted mode is faster than compiling for native mode.

When determining if native mode complication makes sense, the following factors apply:

- Native compilation provides the greatest performance gains for computation-intensive procedural operations.
- Native compilation provides the least performance gains for PL/SQL subprograms that spend most of their time running SQL.
- When a significant number of natively compiled units (typically over 15,000) are simultaneously active, the amount of shared memory required might affect system performance.

You can compile a single PL/SQL subprogram using native compilation by using the PLSQL_CODE_TYPE keyword as follows:

```
ALTER PROCEDURE my_proc COMPILE PLSQL_CODE_TYPE=NATIVE
    REUSE SETTINGS;
```

You can also use ALTER SESSION to change the default compilation mode for the current database session to NATIVE. All PL/SQL compiled during that session will use NATIVE compilation unless specifically configured to use INTERPRETED compilation:

```
ALTER SESSION SET PLSQL_CODE_TYPE = NATIVE;
```

Alternately, the entire database can be configured for PL/SQL native compilation by setting the compilation parameter PLSQL_CODE_TYPE to

NATIVE. If this is done, the performance benefits will apply to the PL/SQL packages that Oracle Database supplies. Setting the PLSQL_CODE_TYPE parameter does not affect existing PL/SQL subprograms. It determines the default mode in which PL/SQL will be compiled in the future. The DBA can recompile all PL/SQL modules in the database to NATIVE or INTERPRETED using one of the following Oracle-supplied scripts:

- **dbmsupgnv.sql** -- Recompiles all PL/SQL modules to NATIVE compilation. During the conversion, TYPE specifications are not recompiled because they do not contain executable code. Package specifications seldom contain executable code so the runtime benefits of compiling to NATIVE are not measurable. You can use the TRUE command-line parameter to exclude package specifications from recompilation to save time.
- **dbmsupgin.sql** -- Recompiles all PL/SQL modules to INTERPRETED compilation. This script does not accept any parameters and does not exclude any PL/SQL units.

Tune PL/SQL code

There are a number of different areas that can provide candidate methods for improving the performance of your PL/SQL code. In an ideal universe, you will always write code to take advantage of the concepts detailed in this section. When that doesn't happen or when you are tuning legacy code written by someone else, the following classes of PL/SQL code are prime candidates for tuning:

- Legacy code that does not take advantage of new PL/SQL language features.
- Dynamic SQL statements written with the DBMS_SQL package.
- Code that spends much time processing SQL statements.
- Functions invoked in queries, which might run millions of times.
- Code that spends much time looping through query results.
- Code that does many numeric computations.

New PL/SQL language features

The following list of features introduced in Oracle 11G have the potential to improve the performance of PL/SQL subprograms where appropriate:

- **DBMS_PARALLEL_EXECUTE** -- This package allows you to incrementally update the data in a large table in parallel. Using this process is recommended whenever you are updating a lot of data. Processing the update in parallel improves performance, reduces the rollback space required, and reduces the number of row locks held. The update is performed in two high-level steps:
    1. Group sets of rows in the table into smaller chunks.
    2. Apply the UPDATE operation to the chunks in parallel. Each chunk is committed after being processed.
- **SIMPLE_* Data Types** -- The SIMPLE_INTEGER, SIMPLE_FLOAT, and SIMPLE_DOUBLE data types are predefined subtypes of PLS_INTEGER, BINARY_FLOAT, and BINARY_DOUBLE, respectively. They each have the same range as its base type, but they include a NOT NULL constraint. Eliminating the overhead of checking for nullness and overflow makes these subtypes provide better performance than their base types. The performance difference is significant when PLSQL_CODE_TYPE='NATIVE', because arithmetic operations on SIMPLE_INTEGER values are done directly in the hardware. When PLSQL_CODE_TYPE='INTERPRETED', the improvement is smaller.
- **CONTINUE** -- The CONTINUE statement is a new LOOP operation that exits the current iteration of a loop and transfers control to the next iteration directly. For large loops where the processing is not applicable to all of the iterations/rows, the ability to skip to the next iteration can result in less time spent in the loop.
- **Sequences** -- It is now possible to make use of sequences directly in PL/SQL Expressions. The pseudocolumns CURRVAL and NEXTVAL improve runtime performance and scalability over the legacy "SELECT sequence.CURRVAL from dual" that was previously required. The sequence_name.CURRVAL and sequence_name.NEXTVAL are legal wherever a NUMBER expression can be used.
- **Result Cache** -- Using a PL/SQL function result cache can save space and time. Any time that a result-cached function is invoked with new parameter values, the parameters and the function

result are stored in the cache. If the same function is invoked with the same parameter values, the result is retrieved from the cache. The cache resides in a shared global area (SGA) and is available to any session that runs the function. PL/SQL function result caching uses more SGA, but less total system memory.
- **Subprogram Inlining** -- Subprogram inlining replaces a subprogram invocation (to a subprogram in the same PL/SQL unit) with a copy of the invoked subprogram, which almost always improves program performance. Individual subprograms can be specified for inlining using the PRAGMA INLINE statement. Alternately, automatic inlining can be enabled by setting the compilation parameter PLSQL_OPTIMIZE_LEVEL to 3 (the default is 2).
- **NATIVE Compilation** -- With release 11G, the PL/SQL Native Compiler Generates Native Code Directly. In previous release, a C compiler was required to generate the native code. PL/SQL developers can now compile subprograms for native execution without any set-up on the part of the DBA.

Tune SQL Statements

For most PL/SQL subprograms, the majority of the execution time is spent on SQL operations. Tuning the SQL statements in the block are therefore a prime candidate for improving overall performance of the program. The full range of SQL tuning options is outside the realm of this guide (or the test). However, the following are common methods for making SQL statements as efficient as possible:

- Use appropriate indexes.
- Use query hints to avoid unnecessary full-table scans.
- Collect current statistics on all tables using the DBMS_STATS package.
- Analyze the execution plans and performance of the SQL statements, using the EXPLAIN PLAN statement and the SQL Trace facility with TKPROF.
- Use bulk SQL to minimize the performance overhead of the communication between PL/SQL and SQL.

Tune Function Invocations

PL/SQL functions that are invoked in queries may get run hundred even thousands of times over the course of a day. Functions where this is possible should be made as efficient as possible. You might be able to minimize the number of function invocations with the use of a nested query. If an inner query filters the result set from the table to a smaller subset of the table rows, the outer query can invoke the function for only that subset.

If a function is being used in the WHERE clause of a QUERY, you should consider creating a function-based index on that table. This can make the query can run much faster because the function value for each row is cached. Without a function-based index, the query cannot use user-created indexes on that column, so the query might invoke the function for every row of the table.

Tune Subprogram Invocations

For subprograms with OUT or IN OUT parameters, it is sometimes possible to decrease the invocation overhead by declaring those parameters with the NOCOPY hint. By default, PL/SQL passes OUT and IN OUT subprogram parameters by value. Every OUT and IN OUT parameter is copied to a temporary variable, which holds the parameter value while the subprogram executes. Once the subprogram completes successfully, the value in the temporary variable is copied back to the corresponding actual parameter. If there is an unhandled exception, the value of the actual parameter is left unchanged. When the parameters in question are large data structures such as collections, records, and instances of ADTs, this copy process slows program execution and increases memory use. For a program does not require that an OUT or IN OUT parameter retain its pre-invocation value if the subprogram ends with an unhandled exception, the NOCOPY hint might be warranted. Using the NOCOPY hint in the parameter declaration requests (but does not ensure) that the compiler pass the corresponding actual parameter by reference instead of value.

Tune Loops

Because loops perform the same step dozens, hundred, or thousands of times each time a PL/SQL subprogram executes, ensuring that loops are optimized is of considerable importance. An operation that takes a quarter-second to complete seems reasonable… until you put it in a loop that will run a thousand times. Ensure that you are only performing operations that you need to in a loop. Ensure that any queries executed in a loop *need* to be executed. For example, if a given query will return the same value each time, then query it and store the result in a variable before the loop starts. Look into SQL set operators that allow you to combine multiple queries. Subqueries that can perform filtering and sorting in multiple stages can also be used to improve performance.

Tune Computation-Intensive Code

These recommendations apply especially (but not only) to computation-intensive PL/SQL code.

- **Use Hardware Arithmetic** -- You should avoid using data types in the NUMBER data type family. The internal representation of these data types is not designed for performance. Operations on data stored in these types will use library arithmetic. Operations on data of the types PLS_INTEGER, BINARY_FLOAT and BINARY_DOUBLE will use hardware arithmetic. For variables that can never have the value NULL, do not need overflow checking, and are not used in performance-critical code, use SIMPLE_INTEGER. For floating-point variables that can never have the value NULL and are not used in performance-critical code, use SIMPLE_FLOAT or SIMPLE_DOUBLE. Many SQL numeric functions are overloaded with versions that accept BINARY_FLOAT and BINARY_DOUBLE parameters. Passing variables of these data types to such functions, and by invoking the conversion functions TO_BINARY_FLOAT and TO_BINARY_DOUBLE can improve performance on computation-intensive code that passes expressions to such functions. Avoid constrained subtypes when creating performance-critical code. Assigning values to variables of a constrained subtype requires extra checking at run time to ensure that the value does not violate the constraint.

- **Minimize Implicit Conversion** -- PL/SQL has the ability to convert between different data types automatically when required. Whenever possible, you should avoid the requirement for implicit conversions. Ways to do this include:
    - ✓ Variables that are to be assigned to or from a table column should be declared as the data type of the column.
    - ✓ Literals should be the same data type as the variable to which is it assigned.
    - ✓ Values from SQL data types that will be used in expressions should be explicitly converted to PL/SQL data types. For example NUMBER values from PL/SQL that are converted to PLS_INTEGER will result in faster arithmetic operations.
    - ✓ When passing values from a variable in one data type to a variable in another, perform an explicit conversion using a SQL conversion function.
    - ✓ Create overloaded subprograms to accept and process parameters of different data types.
- **Use SQL Character Functions** -- There are a number of character functions built into SQL that contain highly optimized low-level code that is more efficient than PL/SQL code. Use the existing functions instead of writing PL/SQL code to do the same things.
- **Put Least Expensive Conditional Tests First** -- A logical expression will stop being evaluated as soon as a result is determined. When the conditions that are the least expensive to evaluate are placed first in logical expressions, the overall time required to execute the expression will decrease. An example would be testing the values of a local variable before testing the return value of a function. If the value of the variable satisfies the condition, then the function will not be executed.

Enable Intraunit inlining

Intraunit inlining is also known as subprogram inlining and it is possible that you might see either term on the exam. Intraunit inlining is an optimization feature that can be conditionally enabled for the PL/SQL compiler. When subprogram inlining is enabled, a subprogram invocation is replaced by a copy of the invoked program when both the invoked and invoking subprograms are in the same program unit. Yes, that's a mouthful... but it is also the definition. Put another way, if you have a PL/SQL block that has a named subprogram declared in its header, inlining affects how calls made within the block to that named subprogram are compiled. When performing subprogram inlining, the compiler makes decisions on the arrangement for the functionality performed by the named subprogram to maximize performance.

The compiler can perform subprogram inlining when the PLSQL_OPTIMIZE_LEVEL compilation parameter is at its default value of 2, or when it is set to a level of 3. When set to 2, subprograms to be inlined must be individually identified by using the INLINE pragma:

```
PRAGMA INLINE (subprogram, 'YES')
```

The PLSQL_OPTIMIZE_LEVEL compilation parameter is used to specify the optimization level that will be used to compile PL/SQL library units. The INLINE functionality is only one of the capabilities controlled by it. The higher the setting of this parameter, the more effort the compiler makes to optimize PL/SQL library units. Generally, the default setting of 2 pays off in better execution performance. If the compiler runs slowly on a particular source module or if optimization is not a factor, then setting this parameter to 1 will result in almost as good a compilation with less use of compile-time resources. The following values and their meaning are:

- **0** -- Maintains the evaluation order of Oracle9i and earlier releases. It also removes the new semantic identity of BINARY_INTEGER and PLS_INTEGER and restores the earlier rules for the evaluation of integer expressions. Level 0 will forfeit most of the performance gains of PL/SQL that were introduced in Oracle Database 10g.

- **1** -- Applies a wide range of optimizations to PL/SQL programs including the elimination of unnecessary computations and exceptions, but generally does not move source code out of its original source order.
- **2** -- Applies optimization techniques beyond those of level 1 including changes which may move source code relatively far from its original location.
- **3** -- Applies optimization techniques beyond those of level 2, automatically including techniques not specifically requested.

When the PLSQL_OPTIMIZE_LEVEL is set to 3, the PL/SQL compiler actively looks for opportunities to inline subprograms. The INLINE pragma is not required in this case, but can still be used to give a subprogram a high priority for inlining. In this case, the compiler will inline the unit unless other considerations or limits make the inlining undesirable. Inlining a subprogram almost always improves performance. Because the compiler inlines subprograms early in the optimization process, subprogram inlining might preclude later optimizations that would have had a greater effect. If subprogram inlining slows the performance of a particular PL/SQL program, you can use the INLINE pragma to turn off inlining for a subprogram:

```
PRAGMA INLINE (subprogram, 'NO')
```

The location of the INLINE pragma is important. It affects only the immediately following declaration or statement, and only some kinds of statements.

When the INLINE pragma immediately precedes a declaration, it affects:

- Every invocation of the specified subprogram in that declaration
- Every initialization value in that declaration except the default initialization values of records

When the INLINE pragma immediately precedes one of these statements, the pragma affects every invocation of the specified subprogram in that statement:

- Assignment
- CALL
- Conditional
- CASE
- CONTINUE WHEN
- EXECUTE IMMEDIATE
- EXIT WHEN
- LOOP
- RETURN

The INLINE pragma does not affect statements that are not in the preceding list.

Improving Performance with Caching

Improve memory usage by caching SQL result sets and using the DBMS_RESULT_CACHE package

In Oracle 11G, a separate shared memory pool called the Result Cache Memory is now available. The result cache stores the results of SQL queries and PL/SQL functions. When these queries and functions are executed repeatedly, the results are retrieved directly from the cache, resulting in a faster response time. The cached results are automatically invalidated when data in the dependent database objects is modified. Because the results are stored in the shared global area (SGA) they are available to all database sessions. The caching mechanism is efficient and requires little change to code or SQL queries to be used. The Result Cache Memory pool consists of the SQL Query Result Cache, which stores the results of SQL queries, and the PL/SQL Function Result Cache, which stores the values returned by PL/SQL functions. Query results that are bigger than the available space in the result cache will not be cached.

When a result-cached function is invoked, the system checks the cache to see if it contains the result from a previous invocation of the function with the same parameter values. If so, the cached result will be returned to the invoker rather than re-executing the function body. If the result for that function with the supplied parameters is not in the cache, the system runs the function body and adds the new result to the cache before returning control to the invoker. If function execution results in an unhandled exception, nothing from that execution is stored in the cache.

The cache can accumulate one result for every unique combination of parameter values for each result-cached function. if the cache runs out of memory, one or more cached results will be aged out to make space for the new result. Because results will be invalidated if any dependant objects are changed, the best candidates for result-caching are functions that are invoked frequently but depend on information that is fairly static.

You cannot cache results when you use the following database objects or functions in your SQL query:

- Dictionary and temporary tables
- Sequence CURRVAL and NEXTVAL pseudo columns
- SQL functions current_date, current_timestamp, local_timestamp, sys_guid, sysdate, and sys_timestamp
- Non-deterministic PL/SQL functions

Parameterized cache results can be reused if the query is equivalent and the parameter values are the same. Cached results are parameterized with the parameter values if any of the following constructs are used in the query:

- Bind variables.
- The following SQL functions: dbtimezone, uid, user, and sessiontimezone.
- NLS parameters.

Result Cache Parameters

- **RESULT_CACHE_MODE** – Determines the default behavior for using the result cache for SQL queries. When set to FORCE, the results of SQL queries are cached by default. When set to MANUAL, a hint is required to enable result cache for a given query.
- **RESULT_CACHE_MAX_SIZE** -- allows you to change the memory allocated to the result cache. The result cache is disabled if you set the value to 0 during database startup.
- **RESULT_CACHE_MAX_RESULT** -- specifies the maximum percentage of result cache memory that can be used by any single result. The default value is 5%, but you can specify any percent value between 1 and 100.
- **RESULT_CACHE_REMOTE_EXPIRATION** -- specifies the time (in minutes) for which a result that accesses remote database objects remains valid. When set to 0 (the default), the SQL query result cache is disabled for queries that access remote tables. Note that when you use a non-zero value, a DML on the remote database will not invalidate the result cache.

DBMS_RESULT_CACHE

The DBMS_RESULT_CACHE package allows the DBA to administer the portion of the shared pool used by the SQL and PL/SQL function result caches. Both these caches use the same infrastructure so DBMS_RESULT_CACHE operations affect both caches simultaneously. The DBMS_RESULT_CACHE package can be used to perform various operations such as bypassing the cache, retrieving statistics on the cache memory usage, and flushing the cache.

- **DBMS_RESULT_CACHE.BYPASS** -- sets the bypass mode for the Result Cache. When bypass mode is turned on, cached results are no longer used and no new results are saved. When bypass mode is turned off, the cache resumes normal operation.
- **DBMS_RESULT_CACHE.FLUSH** -- attempts to remove all the objects from the Result Cache, and depending on the arguments retains or releases the memory and retains or clears the statistics. Prior to flushing the cache, you should set BYPASS to ON.
- **DBMS_RESULT_CACHE.INVALIDATE** -- invalidates all the result-set objects that are dependent upon the specified dependency object.
- **DBMS_RESULT_CACHE.MEMORY_REPORT** -- produces a memory usage report for the Result Cache.

The following dictionary views provide information about the result cache:

- **V$RESULT_CACHE_DEPENDENCY** -- Displays the depends-on relationship between cached results and dependencies.
- **V$RESULT_CACHE_MEMORY** -- Displays all the memory blocks and their status.
- **V$RESULT_CACHE_OBJECTS** -- Displays all the objects (both cached results and dependencies) and their attributes.
- **V$RESULT_CACHE_STATISTICS** -- Displays various Result Cache settings and usage statistics.

Write queries that use the result cache hint

The use of the SQL query result cache can be controlled by setting the **RESULT_CACHE_MODE** initialization parameter. The possible values are **MANUAL** and **FORCE**. When set to MANUAL, you must use the **result_cache** hint in a SQL Query for its results to be cached.

```
SELECT /*+ result_cache */ deptno, AVG(sal)
FROM    emp
GROUP BY deptno;
```

If the result is not already available in the cache, then the query will be executed and the result stored in the cache. Subsequent executions of the statement (including the result cache hint) will use results from the cache. When the RESULT_CACHE_MODE parameter is set to FORCE, all SQL results use the cache by default. Using the **no_result_cache** hint in SQL statements will bypass the cache when using the FORCE mode.

```
SELECT /*+ no_result_cache */ deptno, AVG(sal)
FROM    emp
GROUP BY deptno;
```

When a SQL statement is executed and either contains the RESULT_CACHE hint or RESULT_CACHE_MODE is set to auto, the EXPLAIN PLAN of the statement will indicate that the result cache is being used. The following example enables autotrace and runs a SQL statement with the result cache enabled:

```
SET autotrace traceonly
SET timing on

SELECT /*+ result_cache */
       emp.job_id, dpt.department_name,
       TRUNC(AVG(salary)) avg_sal
FROM   hr.employees emp
       INNER JOIN hr.departments dpt
       ON emp.department_id = dpt.department_id
GROUP BY emp.job_id, dpt.department_name
ORDER BY emp.job_id, dpt.department_name;

21 rows selected.

Elapsed: 00:00:00.19

Execution Plan
----------------------------------------------------------
Plan hash value: 374846896
----------------------------------------------------------------------
|Id | Operation                      | Name          | Rows |Bytes |
----------------------------------------------------------------------
| 0 | SELECT STATEMENT               |               |  107 | 3424 |
| 1 |  RESULT CACHE                  | 345cx7mde5... |      |  ... |
| 2 |   SORT GROUP BY                |               |  107 | 3424 |
| 3 |    MERGE JOIN                  |               |  107 | 3424 |
| 4 |     TABLE ACCESS BY INDEX ROWID| DEPARTMENTS   |   27 |  432 |
| 5 |      INDEX FULL SCAN           | DEPT_ID_PK    |   27 |      |
|*6 |     SORT JOIN                  |               |  108 | 1728 |
| 7 |      TABLE ACCESS FULL         | EMPLOYEES     |  108 | 1728 |
----------------------------------------------------------------------

Statistics
----------------------------------------------------------
         15  recursive calls
          0  db block gets
         12  consistent gets
          0  physical reads
          0  redo size
       1191  bytes sent via SQL*Net to client
        430  bytes received via SQL*Net from client
          3  SQL*Net roundtrips to/from client
          2  sorts (memory)
          0  sorts (disk)
         21  rows processed
```

Operation ID 1 shows that result cache is enabled for this statement. The statistics for the call show that there were 15 recursive calls, 12 consistent gets, and 2 sorts, so Oracle was accessing the data from the data files to get the result. Executing the statement a second time, generates slightly different results:

```
SELECT  /*+ result_cache */
        emp.job_id, dpt.department_name,
        TRUNC(AVG(salary)) avg_sal
FROM    hr.employees emp
        INNER JOIN hr.departments dpt
        ON emp.department_id = dpt.department_id
GROUP BY emp.job_id, dpt.department_name
ORDER BY emp.job_id, dpt.department_name;

21 rows selected.

Elapsed: 00:00:00.01

Execution Plan
----------------------------------------------------------
Plan hash value: 374846896
----------------------------------------------------------
|Id | Operation                         | Name         | Rows |Bytes |
----------------------------------------------------------
| 0 | SELECT STATEMENT                  |              |  107 | 3424 |
| 1 |  RESULT CACHE                     | 345cx7mde5...|      | ...  |
| 2 |   SORT GROUP BY                   |              |  107 | 3424 |
| 3 |    MERGE JOIN                     |              |  107 | 3424 |
| 4 |     TABLE ACCESS BY INDEX ROWID   | DEPARTMENTS  |   27 |  432 |
| 5 |      INDEX FULL SCAN              | DEPT_ID_PK   |   27 |      |
|*6 |     SORT JOIN                     |              |  108 | 1728 |
| 7 |      TABLE ACCESS FULL            | EMPLOYEES    |  108 | 1728 |
----------------------------------------------------------


Statistics
----------------------------------------------------------
          0  recursive calls
          0  db block gets
          0  consistent gets
          0  physical reads
          0  redo size
       1191  bytes sent via SQL*Net to client
        430  bytes received via SQL*Net from client
          3  SQL*Net roundtrips to/from client
          0  sorts (memory)
          0  sorts (disk)
         21  rows processed
```

The execution plan is exactly the same, which seems counter-intuitive. However, the statement is not being reparsed by the optimizer, so this is understandable. However, the elapsed time is smaller. The significant change is in the statistics. The recursive calls, consistent gets, and sorts are all zero. This is because the results were returned from cache rather than re-accessing the data files.

Set up PL/SQL functions to use PL/SQL result caching

A function can be made result-cached by adding the RESULT_CACHE clause to the function definition. If the function is being declared in a package specification, the declaration must also include the RESULT_CACHE option. The following example declares and then defines a result-cached function. When it is first invoked for a given employee ID, the function will query the base tables to populate a record with data for that person. If the function is invoked a second time (and the result has not aged out of the result cache or been invalidated), the record for that employee will be returned from the result cache rather than querying the base tables again. However, if any changes are made (and committed) to either the EMPLOYEES or DEPARTMENTS tables, then all cached results for this function will be invalidated. Calls to a result cached function are identical to calls to an equivalent non-cached function.

```
CREATE OR REPLACE PACKAGE pkg_emp_data
IS
  TYPE emp_record IS RECORD (
        first_name       hr.employees.first_name%TYPE,
        last_name        hr.employees.last_name%TYPE,
        phone_number     hr.employees.phone_number%TYPE,
        department_name  hr.departments.department_name%TYPE);

  FUNCTION get_emp_data (p_emp_id    PLS_INTEGER)
  RETURN emp_record
  RESULT_CACHE;

END pkg_emp_data;
/

CREATE OR REPLACE PACKAGE BODY pkg_emp_data
IS

-- Function definition
FUNCTION get_emp_data (p_emp_id    PLS_INTEGER)
RETURN emp_record
RESULT_CACHE RELIES_ON (HR.DEPARTMENTS, HR.EMPLOYEES)
IS
   v_emp_rec    emp_record;
BEGIN

   SELECT first_name, last_name, phone_number,
dpt.department_name
   INTO   v_emp_rec
   FROM   hr.employees emp
```

```
            INNER JOIN hr.departments dpt
            ON emp.department_id = dpt.department_id
    WHERE   employee_id = p_emp_id;

    RETURN v_emp_rec;
END get_emp_data;

END pkg_emp_data;
/
```

There are several cases in which the body of a result cached function will execute:

- The first time a session for this instance invokes the function with a given set of parameter values
- If the cached result for these parameter values have become invalid.
- If the results for these parameter values have aged out of cache. If space is needed for new entries in the cache, Oracle will remove older entries.
- When the function bypasses the cache. The cache might be bypassed if the result cache has been disabled by a DBA or if a dependent object of the function has uncommitted DML issued against it.

A function must meet all of these criteria to be eligible for result-caching:

- It must not be defined in a module that has invoker's rights
- It cannot be in an anonymous block.
- It cannot be a pipelined table function.
- It must not reference dictionary tables, temporary tables, sequences, or nondeterministic SQL functions.
- It cannot have OUT or IN OUT parameters.
- No IN parameter can be any of these types: BLOB, CLOB, NCLOB, REF CURSOR, Collection, Object, Record.
- The return type cannot be any of these types: BLOB, CLOB, NCLOB, REF CURSOR, Object. It cannot be a record or a collection that contains any of the preceding types.

Oracle recommends that result-cached functions not have any side effects, or depend on session specific settings or application contexts.

Analyzing PL/SQL Code

Run reports on source code

It is often necessary to locate information about existing code, whether your own, or that written by another developer. All PL/SQL source code is stored in the Oracle data dictionary. Querying it is often the best means for getting any information you require. There are four data dictionary views (or twelve, depending on how you are counting) that provide information specific to PL/SQL subprograms. As with many dictionary views, each of the four has three different access levels:

- **DBA** -- Returns rows for all objects in the database.
- **ALL** -- Returns rows for all objects that the current user has access to.
- **USER** -- Returns rows for all objects that the current user owns.

The four base views available are:

- ***_ARGUMENTS** -- Lists the arguments of the procedures and functions.
- ***_DEPENDENCIES** -- Describes dependencies between procedures, packages, functions, package bodies, and triggers.
- ***_PROCEDURES** -- Lists all functions and procedures, along with associated properties.
- ***_SOURCE** -- Contains the text source of the stored objects.

The rest of this section will simply refer to the ALL_ version of the views. However, the other privilege levels could also be used for the same purposes.

The ALL_ARGUMENTS view provides detailed information regarding the arguments of procedures and functions. Essentially every aspect of arguments passed in and out of procedures and functions is provided in this view. You might use this view if you were searching for a particular return value type, or just wanted to see all the parameters for a given package in a single report. A partial list of the columns in this view follows. For the complete list, refer to the Oracle Reference manual.

- **OWNER** -- Owner of the object
- **OBJECT_NAME** -- Name of the procedure or function
- **PACKAGE_NAME** -- Name of the package
- **OVERLOAD** -- Indicates the nth overloading ordered by its appearance in the source; otherwise, it is NULL.
- **ARGUMENT_NAME** -- If the argument is a scalar type, then the argument name is the name of the argument. A null argument name is used to denote a function return.
- **DATA_LEVEL** -- Nesting depth of the argument for composite types
- **POSITION** -- If DATA_LEVEL is zero, then this column holds the position of this item in the argument list, or zero for a function return value. If DATA_LEVEL is greater than zero, then this column holds the position of this item with respect to its siblings at the same DATA_LEVEL.
- **SEQUENCE** -- Defines the sequential order of the argument and its attributes.
- **DATA_TYPE** -- Datatype of the argument
- **DEFAULTED** -- Specifies whether or not the argument is defaulted
- **IN_OUT** -- Direction of the argument:
- **DATA_LENGTH** -- Length of the column (in bytes)
- **DATA_PRECISION** -- Length in decimal digits (NUMBER) or binary digits (FLOAT)
- **DATA_SCALE** -- Digits to the right of the decimal point in a number
- **CHAR_LENGTH** -- Character limit for string datatypes

In the following query, details of all parameters in the PKG_EMP_DATA package created earlier are displayed using the ALL_ARGUMENTS view:

```
SELECT  object_name, argument_name, data_type,   in_out, pls_type
FROM    all_arguments
WHERE   package_name = 'PKG_EMP_DATA';

OBJECT_NAME     ARGUMENT_NAME      DATA_TYPE         IN_OUT PLS_TYPE
-------------   ----------------   ----------------  ------ ------------
GET_MGR_DATA    P_EMP_ID           BINARY_INTEGER    IN     PLS_INTEGER
GET_MGR_DATA    DEPARTMENT_NAME    VARCHAR2          OUT    VARCHAR2
GET_MGR_DATA    PHONE_NUMBER       VARCHAR2          OUT    VARCHAR2
GET_MGR_DATA    LAST_NAME          VARCHAR2          OUT    VARCHAR2
GET_MGR_DATA    FIRST_NAME         VARCHAR2          OUT    VARCHAR2
GET_MGR_DATA    PL/SQL RECORD                        OUT
```

Another means of getting parameter information is through DBMS_DESCRIBE.DESCRIBE_PROCEDURE. This Oracle-supplied subprogram takes the name of a stored procedure and returns information about each parameter of that procedure. Effectively it provides a subset of the information available in the ALL_ARGUMENTS view for a given subprogram.

```
DBMS_DESCRIBE.DESCRIBE_PROCEDURE(
              object_name                 IN VARCHAR2,
              reserved1                   IN VARCHAR2,
              reserved2                   IN VARCHAR2,
              overload                    OUT NUMBER_TABLE,
              position                    OUT NUMBER_TABLE,
              level                       OUT NUMBER_TABLE,
              argument_name               OUT VARCHAR2_TABLE,
              datatype                    OUT NUMBER_TABLE,
              default_value               OUT NUMBER_TABLE,
              in_out                      OUT NUMBER_TABLE,
              length                      OUT NUMBER_TABLE,
              precision                   OUT NUMBER_TABLE,
              scale                       OUT NUMBER_TABLE,
              radix                       OUT NUMBER_TABLE,
              spare                       OUT NUMBER_TABLE
              include_string_constraints  OUT BOOLEAN DEFAULT FALSE);
```

The ALL_DEPENDENCIES view is useful for determining which Oracle objects have dependencies on other objects in the database. When an object that a procedure or function depends upon is altered, that alteration often causes the procedure or function to become invalid either temporarily or permanently. This view describes dependencies between procedures, packages, functions, package bodies, and triggers. A common use of the view is to help verify that a particular object is not referenced by any other objects prior to dropping it. The columns available in this view are:

- **OWNER** -- NOT NULL Owner of the object
- **NAME** -- NOT NULL Name of the object
- **TYPE** -- Type of the object
- **REFERENCED_OWNER** -- Owner of the referenced object
- **REFERENCED_NAME** -- Name of the referenced object
- **REFERENCED_TYPE** -- Type of the referenced object
- **REFERENCED_LINK_NAME** -- Name of the link to the parent object (if remote)
- **SCHEMAID** -- ID of the current schema
- **DEPENDENCY_TYPE** -- Indicates whether the dependency is a REF dependency (REF) or not (HARD)

In the following query, the ALL_DEPENDENCIES view is used to determine all dependencies for the PKG_EMP_DATA package:

```
SELECT type, referenced_owner, referenced_type,
dependency_type
FROM    all_dependencies
WHERE   name = 'PKG_EMP_DATA';

TYPE             REFERENCED_OWNER REFERENCED_TYPE DEPENDENCY_TYPE
---------------- ---------------- --------------- ---------------
PACKAGE BODY     SYS              PACKAGE         HARD
PACKAGE          SYS              PACKAGE         HARD
PACKAGE BODY     HR               TABLE           HARD
PACKAGE          HR               TABLE           HARD
PACKAGE BODY     HR               TABLE           HARD
PACKAGE          HR               TABLE           HARD
PACKAGE BODY     OCPGURU          PACKAGE         HARD
```

The somewhat misleadingly named ALL_PROCEDURES view (it also contains functions, there is no ALL_FUNCTIONS view) contains details about all procedures and functions in the database. You can use this view to determine whether or not a given function is pipelined, parallel enabled or an aggregate function. For pipelined or aggregate functions, any associated implementation type will also be identified. The columns present in this view are:

- **OWNER** -- NOT NULL Owner of the procedure
- **OBJECT_NAME** -- NOT NULL Name of the object: top-level function, procedure, or package name
- **PROCEDURE_NAME** -- Name of the procedure
- **OBJECT_ID** -- Object number of the object
- **SUBPROGRAM_ID** -- Unique subprogram identifier
- **OVERLOAD** -- Overload unique identifier
- **OBJECT_TYPE** -- The type name of the object
- **AGGREGATE** -- Indicates whether the procedure is an aggregate function (YES) or not (NO)
- **PIPELINED** -- Indicates whether the procedure is a pipelined table function (YES) or not (NO)
- **IMPLTYPEOWNER** -- Owner of the implementation type, if any
- **IMPLTYPENAME** -- Name of the implementation type, if any
- **PARALLEL** -- Indicates whether the procedure or function is parallel-enabled (YES) or not (NO)
- **INTERFACE** -- YES, if the procedure/function is a table function implemented using the ODCI interface; otherwise NO
- **DETERMINISTIC** -- YES, if the procedure/function is declared to be deterministic; otherwise NO
- **AUTHID** -- Indicates whether the procedure/function is declared to execute as DEFINER or CURRENT_USER (invoker)

In the following query, the ALL_PROCEDURES view is queried for information on the subprograms in the PKG_EMP_DATA package:

```
SELECT procedure_name, aggregate, pipelined,
       parallel, authid
FROM   all_procedures
WHERE  object_name = 'PKG_EMP_DATA'

PROCEDURE_NAME   AGGREGATE  PIPELINED  PARALLEL  AUTHID
---------------  ---------  ---------  --------  -------
GET_MGR_DATA     NO         NO         NO        DEFINER
                 NO         NO         NO        DEFINER
```

Of the four views in this section, the ALL_SOURCE will be the one you most commonly query (if you are anything like me). This view contains the text source of the PL/SQL objects in the database. This is the view that you will use to answer questions like "I know that I wrote a procedure to perform 'X' functionality. Now what did I call it?" With the exception of WRAPPED packages, this view will allow you to do full-text searches of all the code in the data dictionary. The columns in the ALL_SOURCE view are:

- **OWNER** -- NOT NULL Owner of the object
- **NAME** -- NOT NULL Name of the object
- **TYPE** -- Type of object: FUNCTION, JAVA SOURCE, PACKAGE, PACKAGE BODY, PROCEDURE, TRIGGER, TYPE, TYPE BODY
- **LINE** -- Line number of this line of source
- **TEXT** -- Text source of the stored object

The following query searches the ALL_SOURCE view for all text lines containing the text 'MGR_RECORD'. The result shows that the record is in the PKG_EMP_DATA package and what lines it appears in.

```
SELECT name, type, line, text
FROM   all_source
WHERE  UPPER(text) LIKE '%MGR_RECORD%';

NAME             TYPE            LINE TEXT
---------------  --------------  ---- ------------------------------
PKG_EMP_DATA     PACKAGE            3 TYPE mgr_record IS RECORD (
PKG_EMP_DATA     PACKAGE           10 RETURN mgr_record
PKG_EMP_DATA     PACKAGE BODY       6 RETURN mgr_record
PKG_EMP_DATA     PACKAGE BODY       9 v_emp_rec    mgr_record;
```

Determine identifier types and usages

PL/Scope is a new tool with 11G that uses PL/SQL source text to collect data about user-defined identifiers. PL/Scope is often used through interactive development environments such as SQL Developer. It allows for the development of source text browsers that minimize the time spent browsing through source text in order to understand it. The data collected by PL/Scope is stored in the SYSAUX tablespace. If the SYSAUX tablespace is unavailable, PL/Scope will not collect any data. The compiler will not issue a warning, but a warning will be saved in USER_ERRORS.

In order for PL/Scope to collect data for all identifiers in the PL/SQL source program, the PL/SQL compilation parameter PLSCOPE_SETTINGS must be set to 'IDENTIFIERS:ALL'. The default value for this parameter is 'IDENTIFIERS:NONE'. This parameter can be set at three levels:

- **System** – When the ALTER SYSTEM command is used to change the parameter, all PL/SQL compiled in the database will save the identifiers by default.
  ```
  ALTER SYSTEM SET PLSCOPE_SETTINGS = 'IDENTIFIERS:ALL';
  ```

- **Session** – When the ALTER SESSION command is used to change the parameter, all PL/SQL compiled in the current session will save the identifiers by default.
  ```
  ALTER SESSION SET PLSCOPE_SETTINGS = 'IDENTIFIERS:ALL';
  ```

- **Object** – When a PL/SQL object is compiled, the parameter can be set and will be in effect for that object only.
  ```
  ALTER PROCEDURE get_emp_data COMPILE
  PLSCOPE_SETTINGS = 'IDENTIFIERS:ALL';
  ```

You can determine what PL/SCOPE flag a given object was compiled under via the *_PLSQL_OBJECT_SETTINGS views:

```
SELECT TYPE, PLSQL_CODE_TYPE, PLSQL_DEBUG, PLSCOPE_SETTINGS
FROM    user_plsql_object_settings
WHERE   name = 'GET_EMP_DATA';

TYPE            PLSQL_CODE_TYPE PLSQL_DEBUG  PLSCOPE_SETTINGS
-----------     --------------- -----------  ----------------
PROCEDURE       INTERPRETED     TRUE         IDENTIFIERS:ALL
```

The data collected by PL/SCOPE can be retrieved with the static data dictionary views *_IDENTIFIERS. The columns in the ALL_IDENTIFIERS VIEW are:

- **OWNER** -- Owner of the identifier
- **NAME** -- Name of the identifier
- **SIGNATURE** -- Signature of the identifier
- **TYPE** -- Type of the identifier

- **OBJECT_NAME** -- Name of the object where the identifier action occurred
- **OBJECT_TYPE** -- Type of the object where the identifier action occurred
- **USAGE** -- Type of the identifier usage: (DECLARATION, DEFINITION, CALL, REFERENCE, ASSIGNMENT)
- **USAGE_ID** -- Unique key for the identifier usage within the object
- **LINE** -- Line number of the identifier action
- **COL** -- Column number of the identifier action
- **USAGE_CONTEXT_ID** -- Context USAGE_ID of the identifier usage

There are several identifier usages that PL/Scope Reports in the USAGE column of the *_IDENTIFIER static data dictionary views:

- **ASSIGNMENT** -- An assignment can be made only to an identifier that can have a value, such as a VARIABLE.
- **CALL** -- A CALL is an operation that pushes a call onto the call stack.
- **DECLARATION** -- A DECLARATION tells the compiler that an identifier exists, and each identifier has exactly one DECLARATION. Each DECLARATION can have an associated data type.
- **DEFINITION** -- A DEFINITION tells the compiler how to implement or use a previously declared identifier.
- **REFERENCE** -- A REFERENCE uses an identifier without changing its value.

In the following example, the PLSCOPE_SETTINGS parameter is set to IDENTIFIERS:ALL for the current session. The PKG_EMP_DATA package is recompiled, and then the contents of the ALL_IDENTIFIERS view for that package is queried:

```
ALTER SESSION SET PLSCOPE_SETTINGS='IDENTIFIERS:ALL';
ALTER PACKAGE pkg_emp_data COMPILE;
```

```
SELECT name, type, usage, usage_id, line, col
FROM   all_identifiers
WHERE  object_name='PKG_EMP_DATA';

NAME                 TYPE          USAGE         USAGE_ID LINE COL
-----------------    -----------   -----------   -------- ---- ---
MGR_RECORD           RECORD        REFERENCE           10   10  10
PLS_INTEGER          SUBTYPE       REFERENCE            9    9  39
P_EMP_ID             FORMAL IN     DECLARATION          8    9  26
GET_MGR_DATA         FUNCTION      DECLARATION          7    9  12
DEPARTMENT_NAME      VARIABLE      DECLARATION          6    7  10
PHONE_NUMBER         VARIABLE      DECLARATION          5    6  10
LAST_NAME            VARIABLE      DECLARATION          4    5  10
FIRST_NAME           VARIABLE      DECLARATION          3    4  10
MGR_RECORD           RECORD        DECLARATION          2    3   8
PKG_EMP_DATA         PACKAGE       DECLARATION          1    1   9
V_EMP_REC            VARIABLE      REFERENCE           10   20  10
V_EMP_REC            VARIABLE      ASSIGNMENT           9   13  10
P_EMP_ID             FORMAL IN     REFERENCE            8   17  24
MGR_RECORD           RECORD        REFERENCE            7    9  15
V_EMP_REC            VARIABLE      DECLARATION          6    9   3
MGR_RECORD           RECORD        REFERENCE            5    6   8
PLS_INTEGER          SUBTYPE       REFERENCE            4    5  37
P_EMP_ID             FORMAL IN     DECLARATION          3    5  24
GET_MGR_DATA         FUNCTION      DEFINITION           2    5  10
PKG_EMP_DATA         PACKAGE       DEFINITION           1    1  14
```

Use DBMS_METADATA to retrieve object definitions

The DBMS_METADATA package is a method for retrieving the metadata for data dictionary objects. The most common usage of the package is using it to get the SQL required to recreate data dictionary objects such as tables, users, tablespaces, etc. It is possible to retrieve the metadata and perform transformations on it (such as adding columns to a table)

The following DBMS_METADATA subprograms are used for retrieving multiple objects from the database:

- **ADD_TRANSFORM** -- Specifies a transform that FETCH_xxx applies to the XML representation of the retrieved objects
- **CLOSE** -- Invalidates the handle returned by OPEN and cleans up the associated state
- **FETCH_xxx** -- Returns metadata for objects meeting the criteria established by OPEN, SET_FILTER, SET_COUNT, ADD_TRANSFORM, and so on

- **GET_QUERY** -- Returns the text of the queries that are used by FETCH_xxx
- **GET_xxx** -- Fetches the metadata for a specified object as XML, SXML, or DDL, using only a single call
- **OPEN** -- Specifies the type of object to be retrieved, the version of its metadata, and the object model
- **SET_COUNT** -- Specifies the maximum number of objects to be retrieved in a single FETCH_xxx call
- **SET_FILTER** -- Specifies restrictions on the objects to be retrieved, for example, the object name or schema
- **SET_PARSE_ITEM** -- Enables output parsing by specifying an object attribute to be parsed and returned
- **SET_TRANSFORM_PARAM** -- Specifies parameters to the XSLT stylesheets identified by transform_handle
- **SET_REMAP_PARAM** -- Specifies parameters to the XSLT stylesheets identified by transform_handle

Two of the more commonly used functions in the DBMS_METADATA package are the GET_DDL and GET_DEPENDENT_DDL functions shown below. GET_DDL retrieves the DDL for a single database object whereas GET_DEPENDANT_DDL will return the DDL for one or more dependant objects.

```
FUNCTION get_ddl (
   object_type         IN VARCHAR2,
   name                IN VARCHAR2,
   schema              IN VARCHAR2 DEFAULT NULL,
   version             IN VARCHAR2 DEFAULT 'COMPATIBLE',
   model               IN VARCHAR2 DEFAULT 'ORACLE',
   transform           IN VARCHAR2 DEFAULT NULL)
RETURN CLOB;

FUNCTION get_dependent_ddl (
   object_type         IN VARCHAR2,
   base_object_name    IN VARCHAR2,
   base_object_schema  IN VARCHAR2 DEFAULT NULL,
   version             IN VARCHAR2 DEFAULT 'COMPATIBLE',
   model               IN VARCHAR2 DEFAULT 'ORACLE',
   transform           IN VARCHAR2 DEFAULT 'DDL',
   object_count        IN NUMBER   DEFAULT 10000)
RETURN CLOB;
```

The following SELECT statement uses the DBMS_METADATA.GET_DDL function to return the DDL to create several sequences:

```
SELECT  dbms_metadata.get_ddl (object_type, object_name, USER)
FROM    user_objects
WHERE   object_type LIKE 'SEQUENCE'
AND     object_name LIKE '%AEB%';

CREATE SEQUENCE "OCP"."SEQ_AEB_APPS"
  MINVALUE 1 MAXVALUE 9999999999999999999999999999
  INCREMENT BY 1 START WITH 2
  NOCACHE  NOORDER  NOCYCLE ;

CREATE SEQUENCE  "OCP"."SEQ_AEB_COLUMNS"
  MINVALUE 1 MAXVALUE 9999999999999999999999999999
  INCREMENT BY 1 START WITH 79
  NOCACHE  NOORDER  NOCYCLE ;

CREATE SEQUENCE  "OCP"."SEQ_AEB_TABLES"
  MINVALUE 1 MAXVALUE 9999999999999999999999999999
  INCREMENT BY 1 START WITH 14
  NOCACHE  NOORDER  NOCYCLE ;
```

The subprograms in the DBMS_METADATA package allow you to pull the metadata from the data dictionary for a targeted set of objects. You can perform transformations on them automatically, changing users, tablespaces, constraints, and more. The example below pulls a single table from the OCPGURU schema, remaps the schema name, and outputs the DDL.

```
DECLARE
    v_hnd       NUMBER;
    v_th        NUMBER;
    v_sql       CLOB;
BEGIN
    v_hnd := DBMS_METADATA.OPEN('TABLE');
    DBMS_METADATA.SET_FILTER(v_hnd, 'SCHEMA','OCPGURU');
    DBMS_METADATA.SET_FILTER (v_hnd, 'NAME','AIRCRAFT_TYPES');

    v_th := DBMS_METADATA. ADD_TRANSFORM (v_hnd,'MODIFY');
    DBMS_METADATA.SET_REMAP_PARAM(v_th,'REMAP_SCHEMA','HR','TOM');

    v_th := DBMS_METADATA.ADD_TRANSFORM(v_hnd,'DDL');
    DBMS_METADATA.SET_TRANSFORM_PARAM(v_th,'SEGMENT_ATTRIBUTES',false);

    v_sql := DBMS_METADATA.FETCH_CLOB(v_hnd);
    DBMS_METADATA.close(v_hnd);

    DBMS_OUTPUT.PUT_LINE(v_sql);
END;


  CREATE TABLE "OCPGURU"."AIRCRAFT_TYPES"
   ( "ACT_ID" NUMBER,
     "ACT_NAME" VARCHAR2(12),
     "ACT_BODY_STYLE" VARCHAR2(10),
     "ACT_DECKS" VARCHAR2(10),
     "ACT_SEATS" NUMBER NOT NULL ENABLE,
      PRIMARY KEY ("ACT_ID") ENABLE
   )
```

DBMS_METADATA has a huge number of options and capabilities that allow it to filter the data returned and perform transformations on it. It is part of the back-end of Oracle's Data Pump tool. The PL/SQL Packages and Types Reference contains more detailed information on the full features of this package.

Profiling and Tracing PL/SQL Code

Trace PL/SQL program execution

The DBMS_TRACE package allows you to trace the execution of individual lines of code by subprogram. The trace statistics collected by the package are saved to a pair of database tables which can then be queried to perform your analysis. It is possible to limit the types of lines to be traced, calls to functions and procedures only, exceptions, SQL statements, or any combination of these. Trace sessions do not overwrite earlier results so it is possible to compare traces from different time periods. The DBMS_TRACE package is installed by default in Oracle 11G. However, if the package does not exist in your install for some reason, it can be created by executing the following two scripts while connected as the SYS user:

- **dbmspbt.sql** -- Package specification for PL/SQL tracing
- **prvtpbt.sql** -- This script creates the DBMS_TRACE package body

DBMS_TRACE will write trace information out to a pair of tables that are stored in the SYS schema. These tables are not installed by default and must be created by running the tracetab.sql script as the SYS user. You then need to create public synonyms for the tables and privileges on the tables to allow database users other than SYS to store and retrieve trace data. The objects created by the script are:

- **PLSQL_TRACE_RUNS** -- Table to store run-specific information for the PL/SQL trace.
- **PLSQL_TRACE_EVENTS** -- Table to store accumulated data from all trace runs.
- **PLSQL_TRACE_RUNNUMBER** -- A sequence used to generate unique trace run numbers.

After running the tracetab.sql script, you should perform the following actions to make the tables available. The grants here are made to PUBLIC.

A much better security model would be to grant the privileges to specific users or roles that need to run DBMS_TRACE.

```
CREATE PUBLIC SYNONYM plsql_trace_runs
  FOR plsql_trace_runs;
CREATE PUBLIC SYNONYM plsql_trace_events
  FOR plsql_trace_events;
CREATE PUBLIC SYNONYM plsql_trace_runnumber
  FOR plsql_trace_runnumber;
GRANT SELECT, INSERT, UPDATE, DELETE
  ON plsql_trace_runs TO PUBLIC;
GRANT SELECT, INSERT, UPDATE, DELETE
  ON plsql_trace_events TO PUBLIC;
GRANT SELECT
  ON plsql_trace_runnumber TO PUBLIC;
```

The basic process to trace a PL/SQL subprogram is:

1. Limit DBMS_TRACE to a specific set of subprograms and choose an appropriate tracing level. If you do not set limits on the trace session, the result can generate enough data that it will be difficult to analyze.
2. Begin a tracing session.
3. Execute the PL/SQL subprogram(s) that are to be traced.
4. Stop the tracing session.

At this point, the data for that tracing session will be in the PLSQL_TRACE_RUNS and PLSQL_TRACE_EVENTS tables. You can use the data in these tables to analyze the performance of the target subprogram(s).

Some of the key tracing features are:

- **Tracing Calls** -- Provides output when one PL/SQL program calls another. It is possible to trace every call (TRACE_ALL_CALLS) or only those for "enabled" subprograms (TRACE_ENABLED_CALLS).
- **Tracing Exceptions** -- Provides output when an exception is raised. It is possible to trace every exception (TRACE_ALL_EXCEPTIONS) or only those for "enabled" subprograms (TRACE_ENABLED_CALLS).

- **Tracing SQL** -- Provides output when SQL is issued from within the subprograms. It is possible to trace every exception (TRACE_ALL_SQL) or only those for "enabled" subprograms (TRACE_ENABLED_SQL).
- **Tracing Lines** -- Provides output for the execution of individual lines of PL/SQL. It is possible to trace every exception (TRACE_ALL_LINES) or only those for "enabled" subprograms (TRACE_ENABLED_LINES).

When tracing has been requested for enabled program units only, no trace data will be written if the current program unit is not enabled. Calls to DBMS_TRACE.SET_PLSQL_TRACE and DBMS_TRACE.CLEAR_PLSQL_TRACE store a special trace record in the database. This allows you to determine when trace settings were changed.

Tracing can be limited only to specific subprograms by using one of the ENABLED options. An existing subprogram program can have trace enabled using one of the following methods:

1. Set the PLSQL_DEBUG parameter at the session level and recompile the subprogram:
   ```
   ALTER SESSION SET PLSQL_DEBUG=TRUE;
   ALTER PROCEDURE simple_procedure COMPILE;
   ```

2. Compile the subprogram with the DEBUG keyword:
   ```
   ALTER PROCEDURE simple_procedure COMPILE DEBUG;
   ```

It is possible to pause and resume the trace process using the constants TRACE_PAUSE and TRACE_RESUME. No information is gathered while the trace is paused. A trace entry will be generated to indicate that the trace was paused and another when it is resumed. Setting the constant TRACE_LIMIT will cause Oracle to retain only the last 8,192 trace events of a run. This prevents tracing sessions from growing in an uncontrolled fashion. The number is not exact because the line count is not checked on every trace record. Up to 1,000 additional records may be generated. It is also possible to alter the row count with the use of an event. Setting event 10940 to level n changes the record limit to 1024 * n.

The available DBMS_TRACE subprograms are:

- **CLEAR_PLSQL_TRACE** -- Stops trace data dumping in session
- **GET_PLSQL_TRACE_LEVEL** -- Gets the trace level
- **PLSQL_TRACE_VERSION** -- Gets the version number of the trace package
- **SET_PLSQL_TRACE** -- Starts tracing in the current session

In the following example, a trace session is run on what is just about the most simple procedure imaginable (if we exclude BEGIN NULL; END; from consideration). A tracing session using TRACE_ALL_LINES is run against it to demonstrate both how a trace is performed and how much output DBMS_TRACE generates:

```
CREATE OR REPLACE PROCEDURE simple_procedure
IS
BEGIN
  DBMS_OUTPUT.PUT_LINE('I am but a simple procedure');
END;

BEGIN
  DBMS_TRACE.set_plsql_trace (DBMS_TRACE.trace_all_lines);
  simple_procedure;
  DBMS_TRACE.clear_plsql_trace;
END;

SELECT e.event_seq AS SEQ,
       TO_CHAR(e.event_time, 'DD-MON HH24:MI:SS') AS event_time,
       e.event_unit_owner AS OWNER,
       e.event_unit AS UNIT,
       e.event_comment
FROM   plsql_trace_events e
WHERE  e.runid = 1
ORDER BY e.runid, e.event_seq;

SEQ EVENT_TIME       OWNER    UNIT              EVENT_COMMENT
--- ---------------- -------- ----------------- --------------------
  1 14-FEB 23:27:17                             Trace Tool started
  2 14-FEB 23:27:17                             Trace flags changed
  3 14-FEB 23:27:17  SYS      DBMS_TRACE        New line executed
  4 14-FEB 23:27:17  SYS      DBMS_TRACE        New line executed
  5 14-FEB 23:27:17  SYS      DBMS_TRACE        New line executed
  6 14-FEB 23:27:17  SYS      DBMS_TRACE        New line executed
  7 14-FEB 23:27:17           <anonymous>       New line executed
  8 14-FEB 23:27:17  OCPGURU  SIMPLE_PROCEDURE  New line executed
  9 14-FEB 23:27:17  OCPGURU  SIMPLE_PROCEDURE  New line executed
```

```
10  14-FEB 23:27:17   OCPGURU  SIMPLE_PROCEDURE   New line executed
11  14-FEB 23:27:17   SYS      DBMS_OUTPUT        New line executed
12  14-FEB 23:27:17   SYS      DBMS_OUTPUT        New line executed
13  14-FEB 23:27:17   SYS      DBMS_OUTPUT        New line executed
14  14-FEB 23:27:17   SYS      DBMS_OUTPUT        New line executed
15  14-FEB 23:27:17   SYS      DBMS_OUTPUT        New line executed
16  14-FEB 23:27:17   SYS      DBMS_OUTPUT        New line executed
17  14-FEB 23:27:17   SYS      DBMS_OUTPUT        New line executed
18  14-FEB 23:27:17   OCPGURU  SIMPLE_PROCEDURE   New line executed
19  14-FEB 23:27:17   OCPGURU  SIMPLE_PROCEDURE   New line executed
20  14-FEB 23:27:17   OCPGURU  SIMPLE_PROCEDURE   New line executed
21  14-FEB 23:27:17   SYS      DBMS_OUTPUT        New line executed
22  14-FEB 23:27:17   SYS      DBMS_OUTPUT        New line executed
23  14-FEB 23:27:17   OCPGURU  SIMPLE_PROCEDURE   New line executed
24  14-FEB 23:27:17            <anonymous>        New line executed
25  14-FEB 23:27:17   SYS      DBMS_TRACE         New line executed
26  14-FEB 23:27:17   SYS      DBMS_TRACE         New line executed
27  14-FEB 23:27:17   SYS      DBMS_TRACE         New line executed
28  14-FEB 23:27:17   SYS      DBMS_TRACE         New line executed
29  14-FEB 23:27:17   SYS      DBMS_TRACE         New line executed
30  14-FEB 23:27:17   SYS      DBMS_TRACE         New line executed
31  14-FEB 23:27:17   SYS      DBMS_TRACE         New line executed
32  14-FEB 23:27:17   SYS      DBMS_TRACE         New line executed
33  14-FEB 23:27:17   SYS      DBMS_TRACE         New line executed
34  14-FEB 23:27:17                               Trace stopped
```

Most of the output from the trace is not really helpful in analyzing the procedure in question. DBMS_TRACE and DBMS_OUTPUT generated most of the lines. In the next example, the procedure is enabled by compiling with the DEBUG keyword, and a DBMS_TRACE session is run using the TRACE_ENABLED_LINES option. The results from this run are much better targeted to the procedure that was executed.

```
ALTER PROCEDURE simple_procedure COMPILE DEBUG;

BEGIN
  DBMS_TRACE.set_plsql_trace (DBMS_TRACE.trace_enabled_lines);
  simple_procedure;
  DBMS_TRACE.clear_plsql_trace;
END;
/

SELECT e.event_seq AS SEQ,
       TO_CHAR(e.event_time, 'DD-MON HH24:MI:SS') AS event_time,
       e.event_unit_owner AS OWNER,
       e.event_unit AS UNIT,
       e.event_comment
FROM   plsql_trace_events e
WHERE  e.runid = 2
ORDER BY e.runid, e.event_seq;
```

```
SEQ EVENT_TIME         OWNER    UNIT              EVENT_COMMENT
--- ----------------   -------- ----------------- --------------------
  1 14-FEB 23:38:14                               Trace Tool started
  2 14-FEB 23:38:14                               Trace flags changed
  3 14-FEB 23:38:14                               Some NODEBUG events
                                                    skipped
  4 14-FEB 23:38:14    OCPGURU  SIMPLE_PROCEDURE  New line executed
  5 14-FEB 23:38:14    OCPGURU  SIMPLE_PROCEDURE  New line executed
  6 14-FEB 23:38:14    OCPGURU  SIMPLE_PROCEDURE  New line executed
  7 14-FEB 23:38:14                               Some NODEBUG events
                                                    skipped
  8 14-FEB 23:38:14    OCPGURU  SIMPLE_PROCEDURE  New line executed
  9 14-FEB 23:38:14                               Some NODEBUG events
                                                    skipped
 10 14-FEB 23:38:14                               Trace stopped
```

Profile PL/SQL applications

Until Oracle 11G, the DBMS_PROFILER package provided the interface to profile PL/SQL applications in order to identify performance bottlenecks. It is still available and can be used by developers to provide data to focus their incremental testing efforts. It provides information about individual lines of code such as:

- The total number of times it has been executed
- The total amount of time that has been spent executing it
- The minimum and maximum times that have been spent on a particular execution.

The subprograms available in the DBMS_PROFILER package are:

- **FLUSH_DATA** -- Flushes profiler data collected in the user's session
- **GET_VERSION** -- Gets the version of this API
- **INTERNAL_VERSION_CHECK** -- Verifies that this version of the DBMS_PROFILER package can work with the implementation in the database
- **PAUSE_PROFILER** -- Pauses profiler data collection
- **RESUME_PROFILER** -- Resumes profiler data collection
- **START_PROFILER** -- Starts profiler data collection in the user's session
- **STOP_PROFILER** -- Stops profiler data collection in the user's session

DBMS_PROFILE is a non-hierarchical profilers that records the time spent within a given subprogram. This is information is valuable for tuning, but may not be sufficient to spot problems. For example, the procedure FIND_EMP might take a half-second to run. This may seem perfectly adequate if you were not aware that each execution of the LOCATE_EMPS procedure calls FIND_EMP a thousand times. Hierarchical profilers generate results that can provide such information. The DBMS_HPROF package is a hierarchical profiler that was added with Oracle 11G Release 1. Any profiling questions on the exam are almost certain to be about this package rather than the older DBMS_PROFILER. DBMS_HPROF provides a much more robust interface for profiling the execution of PL/SQL applications. Aspects of the package include:

- Reports the dynamic execution profile of a PL/SQL program, organized by subprogram calls
- Accounts for SQL and PL/SQL execution times separately
- Requires no special source or compile-time preparation
- Stores results in database tables for custom report generation
- Provides subprogram-level execution summary information, such as the number of calls to the subprogram, function time, subtree time, and detailed parent-child information.

The PL/SQL hierarchical profiler has two components:

- **Data collection** -- The DBMS_HPROF package provides subprograms to turn hierarchical profiling on and off and write the raw output to an operating system file.
- **Analyzer**-- The DBMS_HPROF.analyze procedure acts as the analyzer component. It processes the raw profiler output and stores the results in hierarchical profiler tables.

The basic steps to collect profile data from a PL/SQL program via the hierarchical profiler are:

1. Verify that you have the EXECUTE privilege on the DBMS_HPROF package and the WRITE privilege on the Oracle directory object where you will store the raw profile output.
2. Execute DBMS_HPROF.START_PROFILING to begin hierarchical profiler data collection for the current session.
3. Execute the PL/SQL program to be profiled for a period long enough to provide adequate code coverage.
4. Execute DBMS_HPROF.STOP_PROFILING end hierarchical profiler data collection for the current session.

The following example profiles the execution of the procedure hprof_test:

```
CREATE OR REPLACE PROCEDURE hprof_test
IS
BEGIN
   FOR v_Lp IN 1..4 LOOP
      simple_procedure;
   END LOOP;
END hprof_test;

BEGIN
   DBMS_HPROF.START_PROFILING('HPROF_DIR', 'hprof_test.trc');

   hprof_test;

   DBMS_HPROF.STOP_PROFILING;
END;
```

The above anonymous block will send raw output from DBMS_HPROF to the file hprof_test.trc. The raw profiler output is intended to be processed by the analyzer component of HPROF. It is marginally readable without the processing, but this is beyond the scope of the test. The analyzer component of the PL/SQL hierarchical profiler, DBMS_HPROF.analyze, processes the raw profiler output and stores the results in the following hierarchical database tables:

- **DBMSHP_RUNS** -- Top-level information for this run of DBMS_HPROF.analyze.
- **DBMSHP_FUNCTION_INFO** -- Information for each subprogram profiled in this run of DBMS_HPROF.analyze.
- **DBMSHP_PARENT_CHILD_INFO** -- Parent-child information for each subprogram profiled in this run of DBMS_HPROF.analyze.

Prior to running the analyzer, these tables need to be created in the schema where the analysis will be made. The schema that will be executing the analyze operation must also have the EXECUTE privilege on the DBMS_HPROF package and the READ privilege on the directory where the raw file is stored. To create the hierarchical profiler tables along with other data structures required for persistently storing profile data, you must run the dbmshptab.sql script. Once you have the proper privileges and the tables exist, you can use the DBMS_HPROF.ANALYZE function to analyze a raw output file.

The following example invokes DBMS_HPROF.ANALYZE against the file created earlier. The function returns a unique identifier that can be use to query the hierarchical profiler tables. The data in these tables allows you to produce customized reports about the execution of the PL/SQL being profiled.

```
DECLARE
  v_hprun     NUMBER;
BEGIN
  v_hprun := DBMS_HPROF.analyze(LOCATION  => 'HPROF_DIR',
                                FILENAME  =>
'hprof_test.trc');
  DBMS_OUTPUT.PUT_LINE('v_hprun: ' || v_hprun);
END;

v_hprun: 3
```

The data available in the three tables for runid 3 follows:

```
SELECT run_timestamp, total_elapsed_time
FROM   dbmshp_runs
WHERE  runid = 3

RUN_TIMESTAMP                        TOTAL_ELAPSED_TIME
---------------------------------    --------------------
15-FEB-13 06.30.30.690000000 PM                     25022

SELECT owner, type, function, line#,
       subtree_elapsed_time AS ST_TIME,
       function_elapsed_time AS FN_TIME, calls
FROM   dbmshp_function_info
WHERE  runid = 3

OWNER    TYPE           FUNCTION          LINE#  ST_TIME  FN_TIME CALLS
-------- -------------- ----------------- -----  -------  ------- -----
OCPGURU  PROCEDURE      HPROF_TEST            1    25022       35     1
OCPGURU  PROCEDURE      SIMPLE_PROCEDURE      1    24987    24983     4
SYS      PACKAGE BODY   STOP_PROFILING       59        0        0     1
SYS      PACKAGE BODY   PUT_LINE            109        4        4     4

SELECT parentsymid, childsymid,
       subtree_elapsed_time AS ST_TIME,
       function_elapsed_time as FN_TIME, calls
FROM   dbmshp_parent_child_info
WHERE  runid = 3

PARENTSYMID CHILDSYMID ST_TIME  FN_TIME  CALLS
----------- ---------- -------- -------- -----
          1          2    24987    24983     4
          2          4        4        4     4
```

The plshprof executable is a command-line located in $ORACLE_HOME/bin/. It can generate HTML reports using either one or two raw profiler output files. The created files can be viewed with any HTML browser. The command to run the plshprof utility is:

```
plshprof [option...] profiler_output_filename_1
profiler_output_filename_2
```

The available plshprof options are:

- **-skip count** -- Skips first count calls. Use only with -trace symbol.
- **-collect count** -- Collects information for count calls. Use only with -trace symbol.
- **-output filename** -- Specifies name of output file
- **-summary** -- Prints only elapsed time
- **-trace symbol** -- Specifies function name of tree root

The following command will analyze and generate an html report called **hp_report.html** from the **hprof_test.trc** file. Since no directory paths are specified, the plshprof executable would need to be in the PATH, and the **hprof_test.trc** file would need to be in the current directory for the below to work:

```
plshprof -output hp_report hprof_test.trc
```

Safeguarding Your Code Against SQL Injection Attacks

Describe SQL injections

SQL injection is a method that is targeted at applications that use client-supplied data in conjunction with code that generates dynamic SQL. Data is maliciously entered into the client application that will alter the SQL to perform operations outside what was intended. If code has not been hardened against such attacks, it may be possible for users to gain unauthorized access to restricted data. There are several different classes of SQL injection attacks, but all of them exploit string input that has not been properly validated. That string input is then 'injected' into a dynamic SQL statement to alter the effect in ways the programmer did not anticipate. The three types of SQL injection are:

- **First Order Attack** -- The attacker can simply enter a malicious string and cause the modified code to be executed immediately.
- **Second Order Attack** -- The attacker injects into persistent storage (such as a table row) which is deemed as a trusted source. An attack is subsequently executed by another activity.
- **Lateral Injection** -- The attacker can manipulate the implicit function TO_CHAR() by changing the values of the environment variables, NLS_DATE_FORMAT or NLS_NUMERIC_CHARACTERS.

Any program or application might be vulnerable to SQL injection. However Web applications are at a considerably higher risk. An attacker can issue SQL injection attacks without any database or application authentication. Web attacks are also easier to perform at a distance and after-hours -- reducing the chances of detection. An attacker's goal in a SQL injection attacks might be gathering sensitive data, manipulating database information, or denial of service. The impact of such attacks varies widely depending on the roles and privileges the SQL statement runs with.

Statement Modification

A dynamic SQL statement is altered so that it runs in a way unintended by the application developer. The most common target of statement modification is performed when an attacker changes the WHERE clause of a dynamic SQL statement in order to retrieve unauthorized data. The easiest means of doing this is by adding a condition to a SQL statement that makes the WHERE clause always evaluate to TRUE. Alternately, the attacker might inject a UNION ALL into the statement to achieve the same goal.

Statement Injection

This attack means that one or more SQL statements are appended to a dynamic SQL statement. Dynamically created anonymous PL/SQL blocks are particularly vulnerable to statement injection. Aside from the dangers of SQL injection, creating an anonymous PL/SQL block from within a PL/SQL block and then dynamically executing it is bad coding practice as a general rule.

Data Type Conversion

It is also possible to make use of NLS session parameters to create a SQL injection attack. Oracle routinely converts information from its internal date format (which is largely unreadable to humans) to a character-based date that makes sense to us. Date information is never stored as a character and never displayed using the internal format, so every single time that a date value is pulled from a table and displayed in character form, or entered fin character form and stored in the table, either an implicit or an explicit date conversion must occur. The model used when converting dates implicitly in both directions makes use of the format models in the NLS_DATE_FORMAT, NLS_TIMESTAMP_FORMAT, or NLS_TIMESTAMP_TZ_FORMAT parameters. The conversion of numeric values applies decimal and group separators specified in the parameter NLS_NUMERIC_CHARACTERS. When the datetime format model "text" is used, then the supplied text is used the conversion result. For example, if the value of NLS_DATE_FORMAT is '"Month:" Month', then in June, TO_CHAR(SYSDATE) returns 'Month: June'. It is possible to use the "text" values from a user-defined NLS_DATE_FORMAT to inject SQL.

Reduce attack surfaces

Reducing attack surfaces is a matter of limiting the potential ways in which your database can be attacked. This includes ensuring that any database privileges that are not required for users to perform their work are revoked and that only those routines that are intended for end-user access are exposed. Performing this task cannot eliminate vulnerability to SQL injection attacks. However, it reduces the potential impact. Some of the key areas that should be considered are:

- **Minimize Access Points** -- When there is no entry point for an application available to an attacker, then it is not possible for them to find a way to use it as an entry point into your system. Minimizing entry points is one of the most effective means to defend against SQL injection attacks. Eliminate any debug, test, deprecated, or other interfaces that are not providing value to the application.
- **Secure Access Points** -- When an entry point needs to exist, make it as secure as possible. If there is a firewall and the access point can be inside it, then it should be inside. When an access point must be outside the firewall, ensure that is makes use of both authorization and authentication techniques.
- **Minimize Privileges** -- The privileges available to users should be the minimum required and not allow them access to any objects beyond those their role justifies.
- **Use Invoker' rights** -- Stored PL/SQL programs should be executed with invoker's rights when possible. The developer accounts creating PL/SQL subroutines generally have a broader range of rights than the users invoking them. If the programs are running using definer's rights, then the ability to execute them grants broader (and more dangerous) rights to the users.
- **Control Data Input** -- Use data types properly. Do not declare a parameter as a VARCHAR2 when it will be used as a number. If

you need only positive integers, use NATURAL instead of NUMBER. Picking the proper data types can reduce the scope of possible attacks, and reduce errors generated by your user base as well.

There are a number of features inherent to the Oracle database that can help in protecting from a variety of attacks, including (but not limited to) SQL injection attacks. Some practices that you should follow include:

- Encrypt sensitive data.
- Evaluate all PUBLIC privileges and revoke them where possible.
- Do not widely grant EXECUTE ANY PROCEDURE.
- Avoid granting privileges WITH ADMIN option.
- Ensure that application users are granted minimum privileges by default. Make privileges configurable if necessary.
- Do not allow wide access to Oracle packages that can operate on the operating system. These packages include: UTL_HTTP, UTL_SMTP, UTL_TCP, DBMS_PIPE, UTL_MAIL, and UTL_FTP
- Certain Oracle packages such as UTL_FILE and DBMS_LOB are governed by the privilege model of the Oracle DIRECTORY object. Protect Oracle DIRECTORY objects.
- Lock the database default accounts and expire the default passwords.
- Remove example scripts and programs from the Oracle directory.
- Run the database listener as a nonprivileged user.
- Ensure that password management is active.
- Enforce password management. Apply basic password management rules, such as password length, history, and complexity, to all user passwords. Mandate that all the users change their passwords regularly.

Use DBMS_ASSERT

The DBMS_ASSERT package provides an interface to validate properties of the input value. It helps you to guard against SQL injection for dynamic SQL that is built via concatenation and that cannot use bind arguments. Generally this means SQL that contains one or more identifiers, such as table names, that are only determined at run-time. The DBMS_ASSERT package contains several functions that can assist in sanitizing input strings, in particular those involving oracle identifiers. The functions available in the DBMS_ASSERT package are:

- **ENQUOTE_LITERAL** -- Enquotes a string literal
- **ENQUOTE_NAME** -- Encloses a name in double quotes
- **NOOP** -- Returns the value without any checking
- **QUALIFIED_SQL_NAME** -- Verifies that the input string is a qualified SQL name
- **SCHEMA_NAME** -- Verifies that the input string is an existing schema name
- **SIMPLE_SQL_NAME** -- Verifies that the input string is a simple SQL name
- **SQL_OBJECT_NAME** -- Verifies that the input parameter string is a qualified SQL identifier of an existing SQL object

In order to determine which of the DBMS_ASSERT functions should be used, it is necessary to understand the difference between identifiers and literals. Depending on the SQL statement, an object name can be either one. In the following SQL statement, EMPLOYEES is an identifier:

```
SELECT first_name
FROM   employees;
```

However, in the following statement, it is a literal:

```
SELECT *
FROM   dba_tab_columns
WHERE  table_name = 'EMPLOYEES';
```

- SQL Literals are verified through the use of the DBMS_ASSERT.ENQUOTE_LITERAL function.
- Simple SQL Names, such as EMPLOYEES are verified through the use of the DBMS_ASSERT.SIMPLE_SQL_NAME.
- Qualified SQL Names such as HR.EMPLOYEES must be converted to a simple SQL name via DBMS_UTILITY.NAME_TOKENIZE() and

then can make use of the DBMS_ASSERT.SIMPLE_SQL_NAME function.

There are several usage guidelines to the DBMS_ASSERT package:

- Do not perform unnecessary uppercase conversions on identifiers.
- When using ENQUOTE_LITERAL, escape single quotation marks in the input.
- Check and reject NULL or empty return results from DBMS_ASSERT.
- Protect all the injectable parameters and code paths.
- Prefix all the calls to DBMS_ASSERT with the owning schema, SYS.

- If DBMS_ASSERT exceptions may be raised from a number of input strings, define and raise exceptions explicitly.

DBMS_ASSERT can help protect an application from some types of malicious input. However, it does not have the ability to identify all attacks. Some of the cases in which DBMS_ASSERT might not be help include:

- Validating TNS connect strings.
- Defending against cross-site scripting attacks.
- Identifying a buffer overflow attack.
- Guaranteeing that a SQL name is in fact a parseable SQL name.
- Protecting against security risks from inappropriate privilege management.

Design immune code

There are several factors in common with all SQL injection attacks. Designing code that is immune to such attacks is a matter of recognizing these factors and preventing the possibility of them being used. SQL injection attacks have the following three elements in common:

- Use of Dynamic SQL that is concatenated with user-supplied input.
- Insufficient validation on the text being supplied by the user.
- Actions being performed which the user does not have privileges for.

The following actions are all designed to reduce or eliminate these three factors. Code that is designed with these concepts in mine can almost always be made immune to SQL injection attacks.

- **Static SQL** -- The use of dynamic SQL is required for a SQL injection attack. If a piece of SQL does not have to be dynamic, then making it static eliminates all possibility of an attack.
- **User Input** -- User input is required for a SQL injection attack. If there is a way to obtain the required information to build the SQL statement without user input, then doing so eliminates all possibility of an attack.
- **Bind variables** -- If you can make use of bind variables to construct the SQL rather than concatenation, this effectively eliminates the possibility of a SQL Injection attack. Oracle makes use of the bind variable values exclusively, without interpreting their contents in any fashion. Bind variables also improve system performance by making SQL more reusable.
- **Validate** -- When it is required that dynamic SQL be constructed through concatenation and user input, then you should perform appropriate checks on that input to ensure that it makes sense. If an object name is being passed in, verify that the object exists in the database and that it is one the use should have access to. You can also verify the length is not excessive. Oracle object names cannot be over thirty characters, so an input over that is automatically invalid. Checking the input length is a simple way to defeat many potential SQL injection attacks. The DBMS_ASSERT package mentioned in the previous section is another useful means for validating user input.
- **Explicit Format Models** -- When accepting user input that contains date or numeric values, make use of explicit conversion functions to convert them to the proper data type. Use of explicit conversion with a supplied format model eliminates any

possibility of maliciously altered NLS parameters being used to produce an injection attack. They also insure that any extra text supplied with the user input will cause the conversion to fail rather than causing the SQL to run with unexpected results.

- **Avoid Privilege Escalation** -- Whenever possible, procedures should be run with invoker's rights. This ensures that even if a SQL injection attack were to get through (for example if 'DELETE * FROM employees' were successfully injected), it would fail unless the user actually had DELETE privileges on the employees table.

- **Avoid Filter Parameters** – When a SQL statement is dynamically constructed where the entire WHERE clause is constructed from user-supplied input, this is known as a filter parameter. Making use of this is extremely bad coding practice. Protect from SQL injection when this is done is extremely difficult. In most cases, you will be unable to determine from within the procedure that the SQL should not be executed. You must make use of secondary protections such as database privileges to prevent the SQL from succeeding after the subprogram submits it for execution. This is far from an ideal solution.

- **Trap Exceptions** -- Any time that invalid user input causes an exception, that exception should be trapped before an unhandled exception message reaches the user. If an attacker sees the Oracle error generated by invalid input, it provides them a window into the code that they can use to assist their efforts to create a successful exploit. It also provides them with notice that the code was poorly written and an exploit may be possible. Providing an informative, but innocuous error message to the user such as 'That is not a valid table name' lets users know that the data supplied was invalid, but gives no clue to attackers how the code is written.

Test code for SQL injection flaws

No single testing strategy will ensure that your code has no vulnerabilities to SQL injection attacks. There are several different actions you can perform that will significantly reduce the possibility that your code has holes that can be exploited by attackers. You should combine several testing techniques to determine with a reasonable amount of confidence that your code is safe to deploy. There are two primary classes of testing:

- **Static Testing** -- This is testing that is performed via code reviews or walkthroughs.
- **Dynamic Testing** -- Performed by executing test cases against the application.

Both types of testing should be performed against any application that has a potential for SQL injection attacks. Best practice it to perform static testing first, followed by dynamic testing. The original developer should perform an initial code review of their work. Generally this should be followed by a peer-review of the code. There are also static analysis tools that can be used. Dynamic testing can be performed using fuzzing tools or specifically designed test cases.

Code reviews
Since SQL injection attacks require dynamic SQL, only those parts of the code that generate dynamic SQL are part of this analysis. Indicators of dynamic SQL include any of the following keywords:
- EXECUTE IMMEDIATE
- OPEN cvariable FOR
- DBMS_SQL
- DBMS_SYS_SQL

Once dynamic SQL has been located in the code, the tester should look for good coding practices like the ones mention in previous sections. Bind variables should be used for user input where possible. When this is not possible, user inputs should be properly constrained and verified.

Static analysis tools
Computer software exists that will analyze the code of programs without actually executing them. The specific methods used vary, but all perform checks looking for specific sets of known coding issues. Because the danger of SQL Injection is not so much what exists within the code as what input gets provided at runtime, static analysis tools will be unable to

locate many SQL Injection vulnerabilities. They can, and should be, part of the process of code testing, but they are not sufficient in isolation.

Fuzzing Tools
These tools are designed to generate random data (i.e. 'fuzz') to be supplied as the input to programs that accept user input. Properly designed code should handle this data without failing or performing unwanted actions. If program reacts badly to the random data, this can be identified and corrected. Fuzz testing eliminates preconceptions made by testers about what 'should' be entered into any given field. Fuzz testing will not explicitly help in detecting inputs that are vulnerable to intentional exploits. It can locate inputs that are insufficiently validated. Fixing those validations may have a secondary effect of eliminating a hole that could be exploited. However, it cannot guarantee that a human attacker won't be able to intentionally submit data that will cause a SQL injection attack.

Test Cases
Creating test cases to specifically test for SQL Injection vulnerabilities is ultimately the best way to reduce the possibility that any exist. Unfortunately, it is also the most time-consuming method available. Attackers might spend hours trying various different inputs trying to find a combination that exploits a hole in the code. When testing user input screens that contain multiple parameters, test cases should check for vulnerabilities on each input parameter individually. All inputs except the one being tested should contain valid input. This can mean creating dozens of test cases against a single input screen. It can be a lot of work, but the alternative of having a potentially undetected vulnerability is worse.

ABOUT THE AUTHOR

Matthew Morris is an Oracle Database Administrator and Developer currently employed as a Database Engineer with Computer Sciences Corporation. Matthew has worked with the Oracle database since 1996 when he worked in the RDBMS support team for Oracle Support Services. Employed with Oracle for over eleven years in support and development positions, Matthew was an early adopter of the Oracle Certified Professional program. He was one of the first one hundred Oracle Certified Database Administrators (version 7.3) and in the first hundred to become an Oracle Certified Forms Developer. In the years since, he has upgraded his Database Administrator certification for releases 8i, 9i, 10G and 11G, and added the Application Express Expert certification. Outside of Oracle, he has CompTIA certifications in Linux+ and Security+.

Printed in Great Britain
by Amazon.co.uk, Ltd.,
Marston Gate.